Especially for

....

From

....

Date

....

A Daily Devotional
for Women

Everyday
Encouragement
& Hope

Debora M. Coty
Pamela L. McQuade
Patricia Mitchell

BARBOUR BOOKS
An Imprint of Barbour Publishing, Inc.

Print ISBN 978-1-62416-854-3

eBook Editions:
Adobe Digital Edition (.epub) 978-1-63409-421-4
Kindle and MobiPocket Edition (.prc) 978-1-63409-422-1

Compiled by Kathy Shutt.

Daily devotional entries written by Debra M. Coty, Pamela L. McQuade, and Patricia Mitchell.

Published by Barbour Books, an imprint of Barbour Publishing, Inc., P.O. Box 719, Uhrichsville, Ohio 44683, www.barbourbooks.com

Our mission is to publish and distribute inspirational products offering exceptional value and biblical encouragement to the masses.

Member of the
Evangelical Christian
Publishers Association

Printed in China.

Everyday Encouragement & Hope

I pray that God, the source of hope,
will fill you completely with joy and
peace because you trust in him.
ROMANS 15:13 NLT

This lovely daily devotional offers just-right-sized readings that are a perfect fit for your busy lifestyle. These 365 devotional readings feature themes that are important to your heart—including faith, friendship, joy, love, rest, trust, peace, security, and dozens more. As you move through the pages of *Everyday Encouragement and Hope*, you'll be comforted and inspired every day of the year as you experience the refreshing peace and assurance that can only be found through an intimate relationship with the Master Creator.

Dancing in the Puddles

꙳꙳꙳꙳꙳

And so, Lord,
where do I put my hope?
My only hope is in you.
PSALM 39:7 NLT

They say you can tell a lot about a person's foundation of hope by the way she handles a rainy day. Does she turn into a Gloomy Gussy, wailing, "Oh, woe is me. . ." or does she make the best of a bad situation? A hope-filled person will realize that abundant life in Christ isn't about simply enduring the storm but also about learning to dance in the puddles. So grab your galoshes, and let's boogie!

God's Plan

My dear brothers, take note of this:
Everyone should be quick to listen,
slow to speak and slow to become angry.

JAMES 1:19 NIV

God gives good advice on anger. Often, if we listen carefully and hold our tongues, we don't become angry in the first place. Good communication forestalls a lot of emotional trauma. Hurt emotions often cause us to speak words we regret, simply making the problem worse. So when we feel tempted to anger, let's stop, listen, and hold our tongues for a while. That's God's plan for more peaceful relationships.

Walking Faith

*"Be strong and courageous, and act;
do not fear nor be dismayed, for the LORD
God, my God, is with you. He will not
fail you nor forsake you."*

1 CHRONICLES 28:20 NASB

What a life verse! What a creed to live by! We are assured that our God will never leave us or forsake us. We draw strength and courage from this assurance and are then able to act; to share our faith boldly—without fear—because we are never alone. The Lord God—our God—is with us.

In His Hands

Do not be anxious about anything,
but in every situation, by prayer and
petition, with thanksgiving,
present your requests to God.

PHILIPPIANS 4:6 NIV

Need a sure cure for anxiety? Start praying.
As you trust that God has your best interests
at heart, no matter what situation you face,
His peace can replace concern. God says
there's nothing you need to worry about. Just
put all your troubles in His hands, and He
who rules the universe yet knows each hair
on your head will see that everything works
out right. Are you ready to trust now?

Interior Decorator

*You, O LORD, are a shield
about me, my glory,
and the One who lifts my head.*

PSALM 3:3 NASB

Have you ever caught a glimpse of yourself
reflected in a window and were shocked at the
hangdog image you unwittingly portrayed?
Slumped shoulders, drooping head, defeated
expression? You can straighten your posture
and adjust your face, but if the change doesn't
come from the inside out, it won't stick. God
is our Interior Decorator. Only He can provide
that inner joy that projects outward and lifts
our heads. Invite Him in to work on your
place.

God Is in Control

*"Who of you by being worried can
add a single hour to his life?"*

MATTHEW 6:27 NASB

What does worry gain us? It can't change the
length of our days, except to decrease the
health of our bodies. Ultimately, worry is the
most self-defeating thing we can engage in.
Besides, why should we give in to concern
when God controls our lives? He will always
set us on the right path, so we don't have to
agonize over life's details.

Designer Label

*We wish that each of you would
always be eager to show how strong
and lasting your hope really is.*

HEBREWS 6:11 CEV

Our behavior is always on display and, like it
or not, we are judged by our actions. . .and
inactions. Without an explanation for our
behavior—that we're motivated by faith to
be Christlike—people will make up their own
ideas: Her mama taught her right; she was
just born nice; she acts sweet so everyone will
like her. Isn't it better to be up-front and give
credit to the One we're emulating? Wear the
label of your Designer proudly.

Blessing Others

*We work hard with our own hands.
When we are cursed, we bless;
when we are persecuted, we endure it.*

1 CORINTHIANS 4:12 NIV

God gave Paul many blessings, and the apostle passed them on, even if the recipients didn't seem to really deserve them. Those who cursed him (and they were, no doubt, many) did not receive a cursing in return. Instead, Paul tried to bless them. Do we follow the apostle's example? When we are cursed by the words of others, what is our response?

Inside-Out Love

God has made everything
beautiful for its own time.
ECCLESIASTES 3:11 NLT

Beauty is a concern of every woman to some
degree. We worry about hair, makeup, weight,
fashions. But real beauty can only come
from God's inside-out love. Once we are
able to finally comprehend His infinite and
extravagant love for us—despite our flat feet
and split ends—our heart glow will reflect
radiant beauty from the inside out. Only when
we feel truly loved are we free to be truly
lovely.

Hold on to Hope

The prospect of the righteous is joy,
but the hopes of the wicked come to nothing.

PROVERBS 10:28 NIV

Trusting in Jesus gave you new life and hope for eternity. So how do you respond when life becomes dark and dull? Does hope slip away? When no obviously great spiritual works are going on, do not assume God has deserted you. Hold on to Him even more firmly and trust. He will keep His promises. Truly, what other option do you have? Without Him, hope disappears.

Granter of Dreams

Hope deferred makes the heart sick,
but a dream fulfilled is a tree of life.
PROVERBS 13:12 NLT

As a teenager, I dreamed of one day writing a book. But life intervened, and I became a wife, mother, occupational therapist, and piano teacher. My writing dream was shelved. Twenty-five years later, after my youngest chick flew the coop, God's still, small voice whispered, "It's time." Within five years, the Granter of Dreams delivered over seventy articles and nine book contracts. What's your dream? Be brave and take the first step.

A Godly Example

❧⤙⤚⤙⤚❧

*"Let the little children come to Me,
and do not forbid them; for of such
is the kingdom of heaven."*

MATTHEW 19:14 NKJV

On earth, Jesus loved children. He never shut
them out. Though their youth gave them little
credence in Israel, He saw the faith potential
in them. Certainly the children loved Jesus,
too, for His kindheartedness. Do we shut
children out of our lives because we are too
busy or have more "important" things on our
minds? Then we need to take an example
from Jesus. For a new take on God's kingdom,
spend time with a child today.

Everyday Blessings

*But the eyes of the LORD are on those who
fear him, on those whose hope
is in his unfailing love.*

PSALM 33:18 NIV

The Lord of all creation is watching our every
moment and wants to fill us with His joy. He
often interrupts our lives with His blessings:
butterflies dancing in sunbeams, dew-touched
spiderwebs, cotton candy clouds, and glorious
crimson sunsets. The beauty of His creation
reassures us of His unfailing love and fills us
with hope. But it is up to us to take the time
to notice.

God of Comfort

[God] comforts us in all our troubles, so that we can comfort those in any trouble with the comfort we ourselves receive from God.

2 CORINTHIANS 1:4 NIV

When you hurt, God offers you comfort. No trouble is so large or so small that He will not help. But when you have received His strength for the trouble at hand, do you share it in turn? Comfort isn't meant to be hidden away, but passed on to those in a similar need. As part of the body of Christ, we—the church—should be sharing the knowledge that God cares for and strengthens all His children.

Stop the Roller Coaster

*Why am I discouraged? Why is my heart
so sad? I will put my hope in God!*
PSALM 43:5 NLT

For women, ruts of depression are often
caused by careening hormones. Rampaging
hormones can cause us to spend countless
hours weeping without knowing why—or bite
someone's head off, lose precious sleep, or
sprout funky nervous habits. Knowing that
this hormonally-crazed state is only temporary,
we must intentionally place our hope in
tomorrow and pray that God will turn the
downside up!

Look to the Shepherd

The LORD is my shepherd,
I lack nothing.
PSALM 23:1 NIV

No matter what your physical circumstances, if Jesus is your Shepherd, you never have to want spiritually. No matter what the world throws at you, you can be at peace. No fear overcomes those who follow the Shepherd as their King. He guides them through every trial, leading them faithfully into an eternity with Him.

Are you lacking contentment today? Look to the Shepherd for peace.

My Refuge

*God is our refuge and strength,
always ready to help in times of trouble.*
PSALM 46:1 NLT

What is your quiet place? The place you
go to get away from the fray, to chill out,
think, regroup, and gain perspective? Mine
is a hammock nestled beneath a canopy of
oaks in my backyard. . .nobody around but
birds, squirrels, an occasional wasp, God,
and me. There I can pour out my heart to my
Lord, hear His comforting voice, and feel His
strength refresh me. We all need a quiet place.
God, our refuge, will meet us there.

Watchful Love

*I have learned in whatever
state I am, to be content.*

PHILIPPIANS 4:11 NKJV

Paul wasn't writing about a grit-your-teeth
kind of contentment. He had learned to trust
deeply in God for all his needs, so the apostle
did not worry about future events. His
strength lay in God, who cared for his every
need, even when churches forgot him.

    We, too, can be content in Jesus. If the
boss doesn't give us a raise or an unexpected
bill comes in, He knows it. Nothing escapes
His watchful love in our lives.

Stinkin' Thinkin'

*Let us be sober, having put on the breastplate
of faith and love, and as a helmet,
the hope of salvation.*

1 THESSALONIANS 5:8 NASB

Women's hats aren't as popular as they once
were, but you wouldn't know it by my closet.
I love accessorizing with a perky hat to make
a statement, to disguise a bad hair day, or to
keep my brain from sautéing in the sizzling
Florida sun. The Bible says we need to protect
our minds from bad spiritual rays, too. Nasty
input produces nasty output: stinkin' thinkin'.
When we're tempted to input a questionable
movie or book, let's don our salvation helmets
and say, "No way!"

Our Hope

*God raised him from the dead, freeing him
from the agony of death, because it was
impossible for death to keep its hold on him.*

ACTS 2:24 NIV

Death could not grasp Jesus, the sinless One
who died for the guilty. Though it clings to
sinful beings, it had no claim on God's Son.
Jesus is our only hope. Though sin deserves
death, God's compassion made a way to free
us from its agonies. When we give our poor,
mortal lives to Jesus, we rise in Him, sharing
His eternal life.

Redeeming Pain

✦❧✦

I may have fallen, but I will get up;
I may be sitting in the dark,
*but the L*ORD *is my light.*

MICAH 7:8 CEV

"Life is pain, Highness. Anyone who says differently is selling something." This memorable line from the movie, *The Princess Bride*, rings true. Pain is inevitable in life, but God can use it for redemptive purposes. Pain can knock us down, cast us into darkness, and make us feel defeated. But it's only as debilitating as we allow it to be. We will get up again; we will learn, adapt, and grow through redeeming pain.

DAY 22

God's Promise

*This is the promise that He
has promised us—eternal life.*
1 JOHN 2:25 NKJV

The promise of eternal life comes straight
from God. Those who receive Jesus into their
hearts do not end their existence when they
stop breathing. Their last breath on earth
is merely a precursor of life in eternity with
Jesus. Today you miss the one you lost, and
your heart aches. But in eternity, you will
be reunited and will share the joys of death
conquered by the Savior. Until you meet
again, simply trust in His unfailing promise.

Maid of Honor

*For I fully expect and hope that. . .
my life will bring honor to Christ,
whether I live or die.*

PHILIPPIANS 1:20 NLT

Honor. A word not as respected in our society
as it once was. In these days of suggestive
attire, cohabitation without marriage, and
tolerance for every behavior imaginable, it's
hard to remember what honor means. As
Christians, our hope and expectation is to
honor Christ with our lives—especially in the
details—because we are the only reflection of
Jesus some people might ever see.

The Only Way

*"I am the way and the truth and the life.
No one comes to the Father
except through me."*

JOHN 14:6 NIV

Plenty of people doubt Jesus. But those who
have accepted Him as their Savior need not
wallow in uncertainty. His Spirit speaks to
ours, moment by moment, if we will only
listen. He tells us God has shown us the
way; we need not seek another path or truth.
No other road leads to God. For a vibrant
Christian life, we simply need to continue
down the highway we're traveling with Jesus.

It'll Be All Right

Our comfort is abundant through Christ.
2 CORINTHIANS 1:5 NASB

As children, there's no greater comfort than running to Mommy or Daddy and hearing, "It'll be all right." As adults, when we're frightened, dismayed, or dispirited, we yearn to run to enveloping arms for the same comfort. Abba Father—Papa God—is waiting with open arms to offer us loving comfort in our times of need. If we listen closely, we'll hear His still, small voice speak to our hearts: "It'll be all right, My child."

Compassion

Be merciful to those who doubt.
JUDE 1:22 NIV

If you've ever doubted (as we all have), you can understand why this verse is in the Bible. If well-meaning folks attacked you for your uncertainty, it probably didn't help—they just made you more nervous.

When questions enter our minds, we need someone encouraging to come alongside us and provide answers, not a critic who wants to condemn our feelings. Knowing that, we also need compassion for other doubters. May we be the merciful ones who aid those doubting hearts.

I Am His

My health may fail, and my spirit may grow weak, but God remains the strength of my heart; he is mine forever.

PSALM 73:26 NLT

My dear friend was dying of an inoperable brain tumor. Mother of three, 48-year-old Sherill could no longer walk or care for herself, yet her voice was filled with hope as she gazed unwaveringly into my eyes and quoted this verse. She added something very significant at the end that I'll hold close to my heart and draw strength from when my time comes: "He is mine forever. . .and I am His."

Always Secure

Your throne was established long ago;
you are from all eternity.

PSALM 93:2 NIV

There was never a moment when God did
not exist. No scrap of time or eternity came
into being without Him, and nothing escapes
His powerful reign. That's good news for
His children. For whatever we face, now or
in our heavenly abode, we know our Father
is in control. No spiritual warfare or earthly
disaster lies beyond His plan. No wickedness
of Satan can take Him by surprise. Ours is the
eternal Lord, who has loved us from the start.
In Him, we are always secure.

Increasing Visibility

✦⟡✦

"Where then is my hope?"
JOB 17:15 NIV

On hectic days when fatigue takes its toll,
when we feel like cornless husks, hope
disappears. When hurting people hurt
people, and we're in the line of fire, hope
vanishes. When ideas fizzle, efforts fail;
when we throw the spaghetti against the
wall and nothing sticks, hope seems lost.
But we must remember it's only temporary.
The mountaintop isn't gone just because
it's obscured by fog. Visibility will improve
tomorrow and hope will rise.

Unchanging

*Your word, LORD, is eternal;
it stands firm in the heavens.*

PSALM 119:89 NIV

The Word of God never changes. The Father's
commands do not alter, and neither does
Jesus, the Word made flesh, or His promise
of salvation. Those who trust in Him are
secure as the Lord Himself, for He does
not change, and none of His promises pass
away unfulfilled. The eternal Lord and all
He commands stand firm. To gain eternity,
simply receive Christ as your Savior; then
trust in Him.

Wag More

I am not complaining about having too little. I have learned to be satisfied with whatever I have.

Philippians 4:11 cev

I oozed envy as writer buddies received awards, broke sales records, and snagged lucrative contracts. What about me? Where were my accolades? It had always been enough to know I was following God's chosen path for me, but suddenly all I could do was complain. I wanted more.

Then God sent me a sign. Actually, it was a bumper sticker on a passing car: Wag More, Bark Less. Message received. . .with a smile.

Pure Delight

❧✦❧

You make known to me the path of life;
you will fill me with joy in your presence,
with eternal pleasures at your right hand.

PSALM 16:11 NIV

Rejoicing in God? Those who do not know
Jesus cannot imagine it. You have to know
Jesus to delight in His presence, just as you
cannot enjoy a friend until you come to
know each other and enjoy companionship.
But knowing and loving God brings us, His
children, joy in His presence and the prospect
of undefined pleasures at His side. Are you
prepared to share those joys with Jesus for
eternity?

Lord of the Dance

❧⊱━━━⊰❧

Remember your promise to me;
it is my only hope.
PSALM 119:49 NLT

The Bible contains many promises from God:
He will protect us (Proverbs 1:33), comfort
us (2 Corinthians 1:5), help in our times of
trouble (Psalm 46:1), and encourage us (Isaiah
40:29). The word encourage comes from the
root phrase "to inspire courage." Like an
earthly father encouraging his daughter from
backstage as her steps falter during her dance
recital, our Papa God wants to inspire courage
in us, if we only look to Him.

He Never Fails

If we are faithless, he will remain faithful,
for he cannot disown himself.

2 Timothy 2:13 niv

Sometimes our faith fails, but Jesus never
does. When we change for the worse, slip, or
make a mistake, He is still the same faithful
God He's always been. Though we may falter,
He cannot. If we give in to the tempter's
wiles, let us turn again to the faithful One. If
we have trusted in Him, we can turn to Him
for renewed forgiveness. His own faithfulness
will not allow Him to deny us.

Light My Fire

If God is for us, who can be against us?
ROMANS 8:31 NIV

Some days it feels as if the entire world is conspiring to make us as miserable as possible. Your spouse is crabby, the kids forget to mention the four dozen cupcakes they volunteered you to bake for today, traffic jams, your boss is on the rampage, your coworkers are in nasty moods, you forgot to defrost dinner, the car overheats again. But our God is King of the Universe, and He's on our side. Girl, if that doesn't light your fire, the wood's wet.

Perfection

*His works are perfect, and all his ways
are just. A faithful God who does no
wrong, upright and just is he.*

<small>DEUTERONOMY 32:4 NIV</small>

Many unbelievers, or even weakening
believers living in crisis, complain that God
is unfair. But Moses, who suffered much for
God's people, knew better than that. God
is always perfect, faithful, and just—it's
rebellious humanity that lacks these qualities.

We can have faith in God's perfection.
He's never failed His people yet, though they
have often been false. Trust in Him today. As
He led His people to the Promised Land, He'll
lead you home to Himself.

Acing the Test

*Always be ready to give an answer when
someone asks you about your hope.*
1 PETER 3:15 CEV

Remember algebra tests in high school?
Instant sweat and heart palpitations. You
dreaded going into them unprepared. You
wanted to have answers ready so you wouldn't
be left with saliva drooling from your gaping
mouth when questioned. The Bible says we
should be prepared when someone asks about
the hope within us—the hope they couldn't
help but notice radiating from our souls. The
answer scores an A+ for all eternity: Jesus!

Praise Him

*Let them praise the name of the LORD,
for His name alone is exalted; His glory
is above the earth and heaven.*

PSALM 148:13 NKJV

Trusting Jesus gives you a spectacular
view of God's power. His work in your life
increasingly opens your eyes to this glorious
King who loves you. But those who do not
know Him cannot praise Him. They are
thoroughly blind to the glories of the One
whom they have denied. Yet in the end, His
glory will be apparent even to them. Whom
do you follow—the glorious One or mere
humans?

Chef d'oeuvre

*Be strong and let your heart take courage,
all you who hope in the LORD.*

PSALM 31:24 NASB

_____

Identical eggs can be turned into greasy fried
egg sandwiches or an exquisite soufflé. The
difference is how much beating they endure.

When life seems to be beating us down,
we must remember that we are a masterpiece
in progress. The mixing, slicing, and dicing
may feel brutal at times, but our Lord has
offered us His courage and strength to endure
until He is ready to unveil the chef d'oeuvre.

Building a House

❧❦❧

The wise woman builds her house, but the foolish pulls it down with her hands.

PROVERBS 14:1 NKJV

———————————

Did you know you can build a house? God says so. No, you won't use mortar, brick, and wood. But every Christian woman has the ability to build up her family with her wisdom, industry, and righteousness. Her faithful Christian character blesses those in her home. Today are you building your house or tearing it down? Seek God, and He will help you make it strong.

Superglue Faith

*In Him, you also, after listening to the
message of truth, the gospel of your
salvation—having also believed,
you were sealed in Him with the
Holy Spirit of promise.*

EPHESIANS 1:13 NASB

Remember the old commercial that depicted
a construction worker dangling in midair, the
top of his helmet bonded by superglue to a
horizontal beam? Faith is like superglue. We
cling to our God, our foundation, our beam.
As believers, we are sealed in Christ, and the
bond cannot be undone. Through prayer in
times of despair, our faith is strengthened and
becomes waterproof, pressure-resistant, and
unbreakable.

Parents

"Honor your father and your mother, that your days may be long upon the land."

EXODUS 20:12 NKJV

When we honor our parents, we may not spend much time in the Promised Land, but God will bless us. Treating Mom and Dad well improves our relationships with them and gives our family security. As we treat our children's grandparents well, we model the actions of adult children, and our children are more likely to treat us well, too.

Our Father God has special blessings for those of us who respect our parents. Whether it's Holy Land property or deeper love, He gives us just what we need.

Keep Breathing, Sister!

*As long as we are alive, we still have hope,
just as a live dog is better off
than a dead lion.*

ECCLESIASTES 9:4 CEV

Isn't this a tremendous scripture? At first
glance, the ending elicits a chuckle. But
consider the truth it contains: Regardless of
how powerful, regal, or intimidating a lion is,
when he's dead, he's dead. But the living—you
and I—still have hope. Limitless possibilities!
Hope for today and for the future. Although
we may be as lowly dogs, fresh, juicy bones
abound. As long as we're breathing, it's not
too late!

Appreciation for Mothers

Her children arise and call her blessed;
her husband also, and he praises her.

PROVERBS 31:28 NIV

Wouldn't every woman like to receive this
kind of praise? A few do. Though we all need
praise for a job well done, many families
forget to encourage their members. When we
have followed God faithfully, it shows in our
lives, but we still value others' appreciation.
Has a Christian mother been a wonderful
influence on your life? She'd probably like to
know that. Feel free to share that praise with
others, too.

It's a Mystery

*This is the day which the LORD has made;
let us rejoice and be glad in it.*
PSALM 118:24 NASB

Let's face it, girls, some mornings our
rejoicing lasts only until the toothpaste drips
onto our new shirt or the toast sets off the fire
alarm. But the mystery of Jesus-joy is that it's
not dependent on rosy circumstances. If we,
after cleaning the shirt and scraping the toast,
intentionally give our day to the Lord, He will
infuse it with His joy. Things look much better
through Jesus-joy contact lenses!

Fear Will Flee

*Do not be afraid of sudden terror,
nor of trouble from the wicked when it
comes; for the LORD will be your confidence,
and will keep your foot from being caught.*
PROVERBS 3:25–26 NKJV

What do you have to fear, with God as your
confidence? He protects you from being
snared like a wild animal by the world's
troubles. With His hand over you, no sudden
event or evildoer's plot can destroy you. Give
Him your confidence, and fear will flee.

Going the Distance

[David]. . .chose five smooth stones from the stream. . .and, with his sling in his hand, approached the Philistine.

1 SAMUEL 17:40 NIV

That little dude David had no intention of backing down from his fight until it was finished. Notice he picked up five rocks, not just one. He was prepared to go the distance against his giant. He fully expected God to make him victorious, but he knew it wouldn't be easy.

So you've used your first rock against your giant. Maybe even your second. Don't give up. Keep reloading your sling and go the distance. Victory is sweet!

Fearing God

In the fear of the LORD there is strong confidence, and His children will have a place of refuge.

PROVERBS 14:26 NKJV

There is only one right kind of fear—the fear of God. Not that we need to cower before Him, but we must respect and honor Him and His infinite power. Those who love Him also rightly fear Him. But those who fear God need fear nothing else. He is their refuge, the Protector whom nothing can bypass. Fear God, and you are safe.

Top Off My Tank

"My grace is sufficient for you, for my power is made perfect in weakness."

2 CORINTHIANS 12:9 NIV

There is no weaker vessel than a bedraggled mother at 6 a.m., staring into a bathroom mirror after another rough night. She's trying to decide if the dark smudges beneath her eyes are yesterday's grape jelly when she suddenly realizes she's brushing her hair with her toothbrush. Yep, we are a sisterhood of slightly sagging spiritual warriors, but we can depend on God to power our weak vessels. And He is able.

Secure in the Father

The Spirit you received does not make you slaves, so that you live in fear again; rather, the Spirit you received brought about your adoption to sonship. And by him we cry, "Abba, Father."

ROMANS 8:15 NIV

As part of God's family, you need never dread anything. He who rules the universe adopted you. Since your loving Father no longer condemns you for sin, panic need not rule your life. Fear no retribution, because your elder brother Jesus shed His blood for you, covering every sin. God's child always remains secure in her Abba, "Daddy."

Heavyweight

*This hope is like a firm
and steady anchor for our souls.*
HEBREWS 6:19 CEV

Julia and Mark anchored their sailboat to do
a little reef exploring while they went diving.
When they surfaced, the boat was a speck on
the horizon. It had drifted more than a half-
mile because their anchor was too light.

Hope in Christ is an anchor for our souls.
But if the anchor isn't weighted by firm and
steady faith, we may drift in strong currents of
doubt, problems, and disillusionment. Weigh
your anchor today.

Blessing of Forgiveness

*[Your] sins have been forgiven
on account of his name.*

1 JOHN 2:12 NIV

Who could do something wonderful enough
to earn God's forgiveness? No human work
can buy it. God forgives because of who He
is, not because of who we are or what we do.
That's encouraging, because we can't earn
forgiveness by our own perfection. Instead,
forgiveness becomes the great blessing
of our Christian life that makes living for
Jesus possible. We obey God to show our
appreciation, not to gain entry into His
kingdom.

A Perfect Fit

The LORD is good to those whose hope is in him, to the one who seeks him.

LAMENTATIONS 3:25 NIV

Seeking God is, for some, like a child groping in a dark room for the light switch. She knows it's there, she just can't seem to put her fingers on it. Some search for God all their lives, trying on various religions like pairs of shoes. This one pinches. That one chafes. But we must bypass religious fluff for the heart of the matter: Jesus. The only way to God is through faith in Christ (John 14:6). Suddenly, the shoe fits!

DAY 54

An End to Mourning

*"Blessed are those who mourn,
for they will be comforted."*
MATTHEW 5:4 NIV

How often do we think of mourning as a
good thing? But when it comes to sin, it is.
Those who sorrow over their own sinfulness
will turn to God for forgiveness. When
He willingly responds to their repentance,
mourning ends. Comforted by God's pardon,
transformed sinners celebrate—and joyous
love for Jesus replaces sorrow.

Roots

*"There is hope for your future,"
declares the LORD, "And your children
will return to their own territory."*
JEREMIAH 31:17 NASB

Prodigal. The word alone evokes an
involuntary shudder.

Most of us know parents whose children
have left home in the throes of rebellion.
Some of us are those parents. After years
of protecting and nurturing our children,
heartache replaces harmony, panic supersedes
pride. But the Great Peacemaker declares that
prodigals will one day return to their roots.
One of His greatest parables reinforces that
hope (Luke 15).

Chosen Family

~~~❧❦❧~~~

There is a friend that sticketh closer than a brother.
PROVERBS 18:24 KJV

Family relationships range from the wonderful to the disturbing, and we get whatever God gives us. But we choose our friends based on common interests and experiences. Often this "chosen family" seems closer to us than siblings. Yet neither clings closer than our elder brother Jesus. He teaches us how to love blood relatives and those we choose. No matter whether or not we're related, when we love in Him, that love sticks fast.

Legacy of Love

After all, when the Lord Jesus appears, who else but you will give us hope and joy and be like a glorious crown for us?

1 THESSALONIANS 2:19 CEV

The most hope-inspiring legacy we can pass on to the next generation is faith. What delight it is for us as women to plant and nurture seeds of faith in our children, knowing that at harvest they'll stand by our sides before the Lord Jesus! It's never too late to till the fertile soil of their hearts by our example of daily Bible reading, prayer, and dependence on our Savior.

Prayerful Giving

❧❧❧

Give, and it shall be given unto you; good measure, pressed down. . .and running over.

LUKE 6:38 KJV

Need an example of how to give? Look to God. To those who give generously, He gives overflowing, abundant blessings.

In this fallen world, we need to be careful to whom we give support. Dishonest people or those who oppose God should not be our charitable choices. But many Christian ministries do good work and need our support. Faithful churches need our giving. As we donate prayerfully, God will bless us in return.

His Little Girls

Just as a father has compassion on his children, so the LORD has compassion on those who fear Him.

PSALM 103:13 NASB

Plagued with horrible recurring nightmares during my childhood, I remember the terror of waking up screaming, hair sweat-plastered to my face. Then like a candle in the darkness, my father would appear at my bedside, lie beside me, and gently rub my back until I fell asleep. Our heavenly Father is like that—tender, caring, protective. And He, too, responds when His little girls need comfort from His loving presence.

Want vs. Need

❧❧❧

"Give us this day our daily bread."
MATTHEW 6:11 NKJV

———————————————

Jesus tells us here to ask God for our daily
needs, and we may do that frequently. Let's
remember that even the smallest things, such
as the bread we put on the table, come from
God. Yet have we forgotten that all our food
comes from our heavenly Father? God forgets
nothing we need. So if we don't have steak
instead of hamburgers, could it be because we
want, but don't need, it?

Let the Sun Shine In

"Come to me, all you who are weary and burdened, and I will give you rest."
MATTHEW 11:28 NIV

Nothing chokes hope like weariness. Day in and day out drudgery produces weariness of body, heart, and soul. It feels like dark clouds have obscured the sun and cast us into perpetual shadow. But Jesus promised rest for our weary souls, respite from our burdens, and healing for our wounds. . .if we come to Him. The sun isn't really gone, it's just hidden until the clouds roll away.

Share His Love

"It is more blessed to give than to receive."
ACTS 20:35 NIV

Christmas has become a time of receiving—
to the point where greed motivates more
people than blessing. But Paul reminds us
that getting what we want is not the greatest
blessing. We know that when we see the
delight in a child's eyes at receiving a longed-
for item. Our heavenly Father loves to see the
same joy in our eyes when He helps us in less
tangible ways. That's why He tells us to share
His love with others.

No Wimps Here

*For God has not given us a spirit of fear
and timidity, but of power, love,
and self-discipline.*

2 TIMOTHY 1:7 NLT

Do you suffer paralysis by analysis? Are you so
afraid of trying something new that you put it
off until you can think it through. . .and end up
doing nothing at all? Too much introspection
creates inertia, and we abhor the ineffective
wimps we become. Sisters, God never intended
for us to be wimps. His power and love are
available to replace our fear and infuse us
with courage. Shake off that paralysis and get
moving!

DAY 64

Compassion

*A father to the fatherless, a defender of
widows, is God in his holy dwelling.*
PSALM 68:5 NIV

God's love is very tender toward those who
hurt. Children who have lost their fathers
and women who have lost their husbands
can count on His compassion. When we lose
a loved one, do we focus on the Father's
gentleness? We are more likely to complain
that He did not extend life than to praise Him
for His care. But when we feel the most pain,
we also receive the largest portion of God's
comfort. What hurts His children hurts Him,
too.

When I'm Baaad

"I am the good shepherd; I know my own sheep, and they know me, just as my Father knows me and I know the Father."

<small>JOHN 10:14–15 NLT</small>

Ever spent much time around sheep? They're really self-centered. All they think about is eating, sleeping, and avoiding conflict. But one good thing about sheep is that they'll drop everything and respond to their shepherd's voice. Not anybody else's voice, just the familiar tones of their own shepherd. This little ewe wants to recognize and respond to her beloved Shepherd's voice, too. How about you, ewe?

Simple Words

❧❧❧

Strengthen those who have tired hands,
and encourage those who have weak knees.
ISAIAH 35:3 NLT

A simple word of encouragement or act of kindness can live in memory for years and even a lifetime. You may think someone who holds a high position or appears to have everything under control doesn't need any encouragement, but you never know how unsure of herself or emotionally frayed she's feeling inside. Perhaps your "Wonderful job!" is the confidence booster she's longing to hear. It's possible your thumbs-up is all it will take for someone to know that others notice, understand, and care.

Tolerance Isn't Enough

❧

"In his name the nations will put their hope."
MATTHEW 12:21 NIV

In the summer of 2000, my husband and
I toured the Holy Land. Our Israeli guide
assured us that there was no safer place than
Jerusalem, for people of numerous faiths—
Muslim, Jewish, Christian, Hindu—had
learned tolerance as the key to living together
peaceably. Yet tension was as evident as the
armed guards on every street corner. Violence
erupted three months later with the first bus
bombings. Our only hope for peace is Jehovah.

Children of God

Because you are his sons, God sent the Spirit of his Son into our hearts, the Spirit who calls out, "Abba, Father."

GALATIANS 4:6 NIV

God draws His children near, connecting them firmly to Himself through the Son and the Holy Spirit. There is no division in the Godhead when it comes to loving God's adopted children. With the Spirit, we call out, "Abba, Daddy," to the Holy One who loved us enough to call us to Himself despite our sin. Through Jesus' sacrifice and the Spirit's work, God the Father cleanses us and opens communications so we can follow Him truly.

Questions and Answers

*And the Scriptures were written to teach
and encourage us by giving us hope.*
ROMANS 15:4 CEV

What do you do when facing a perplexing
problem? Ask a family member? Consult a
friend? Turn to the Internet?

God's Word is brimming with answers to
life's difficulties, yet it's often the last place we
turn. God speaks to us today through the lives
of trusting Abraham, broken-hearted Ruth,
runaway Jonah, courageous Esther, female
leader Deborah in a male-dominated society,
beaten-down Job, double-crossing Peter, and
Paul, who proved people can change.

Stand Firm

*The Lord has become my fortress,
and my God the rock in whom I take refuge.*

PSALM 94:22 NIV

Are you under attack by friends, family,
or coworkers? If it comes because of your
obedience to the Lord, stand firm in the
face of their comments. He will defend you.
If you face harsh words or nasty attitudes,
remain kind, and He will assist you. Should
your boss do you wrong, don't worry. Those
who are against a faithful Christian are also
against Him, and God will somehow make
things right.

Hit the Mats

Blessed are those whose help is the God of Jacob, whose hope is in the LORD their God.
PSALM 146:5 NIV

Wrestled with God lately? We all do at one time or another. The Genesis 32 account of Jacob's Almighty wrestling match reassures us that God is not offended when we beat on His chest and shout, "Why?" He understands that we must sometimes wrestle out the mysteries of our faith. Wrestling with his Lord was a turning point for Jacob—he got a new name (Israel) and a new perspective. God is ready to do the same for us.

Our Refuge

The LORD Almighty is the one you are to regard as holy. . .he will be a holy place.

ISAIAH 8:13–14 NIV

When you live in awe of God—when He alone is Lord of your life—you have nothing to fear. If fears or enemies assail you, a place of refuge is always nearby. God never throws His children to the wolves. Instead, He protects them in His holy place. With Jesus as your Savior, you always have a peaceful place to go to.

Girlfriends

And our hope for you is firm, because we know that just as you share in our sufferings, so also you share in our comfort.

2 CORINTHIANS 1:7 NIV

Anne of Green Gables was right: Bosom friends are important. Girls need girlfriends. . .little girls and grown-up girls alike. God wired us to need each other, to yearn for the heart-bonding that results from sharing sufferings, comfort, hugs, and giggles. Nothing's wrong with men, of course, but they don't make the same bosom friends as girls. Have you thanked the Lord lately for your soul sisters?

Receive His Strength

The Lord also will be a refuge for the oppressed, a refuge in times of trouble.

PSALM 9:9 NKJV

The Psalms often speak of God as a refuge. Whether you face something large, like oppression, or something much smaller, He wants you to turn to Him in troublous times. Size does not matter, but your trust in Jesus does. Nothing you face is a shock to Him— He knows your troubles and has not deserted you. So go to your refuge and take strength from Him.

Heaven's Bakery

*"Those who hope in me will
not be disappointed."*

ISAIAH 49:23 NIV

As I stood in line ogling luscious pastries
in the coffee shop's glass case, I asked the
teenage clerk which she would suggest.
Casting cornflower-blue eyes heavenward, she
tapped her dainty chin with one finger before
answering in a wistful voice. "I recommend
the blueberry cheesecake. When I eat it, I
hear angels." What higher recommendation
is there? What greater hope have we than
heaven? (Maybe they'll even serve blueberry
cheesecake there!)

Loving Jesus

*Looking unto Jesus the author
and finisher of our faith.*

HEBREWS 12:2 KJV

God is writing a story of faith through
your life. What will it describe? Will it be a
chronicle of challenges overcome, like the Old
Testament story of Joseph? Or a near tragedy
turned into joy, like that of the prodigal son?
Whatever your account says, if you love Jesus,
the end is never in question. Those who love
Him finish in heaven, despite their trials
on earth. The long, weary path ends in His
arms. Today, write a chapter in your faithful
narrative of God's love.

Beyond the Horizon

❧❧❧

You will be rewarded for this;
your hope will not be disappointed.
PROVERBS 23:17–18 NLT

Have you ever traversed a long, winding road,
unable to see your final destination? Perhaps
you were surprised by twists and turns along
the way or jarred by unexpected potholes.
But you were confident that if you stayed on
that road, you would eventually reach your
destination. Likewise, God has mapped out
our futures. The end of the road may disappear
beyond the horizon, but we are assured that
our destination will not be disappointing.

Spiritual Certainty

We live by faith, not by sight.
2 CORINTHIANS 5:7 NIV

There is more than one way of seeing. We view the world around us with our eyes, but by doing so, we don't apprehend all there is in life. Those things we "see" by faith cannot be envisioned by our physical eyes. That's why doubters disbelieve them. But when God speaks to our hearts, it is as real as if we'd viewed the truth plainly in front of us. Like Paul, though our eyes cannot see it, we have a spiritual certainty.

Kingdom-Purposed Friendship

*"I tell you, use worldly wealth to gain friends
for yourselves, so that when it is gone,
you will be welcomed into eternal dwellings."*

LUKE 16:9 NIV

There is a good way to use the things of the
world, and Jesus describes it here. God has
given us the wealth to share with others,
making use of it to further God's kingdom.
Though we may not have more than a pot of
soup and some bread to offer, they can be the
start of a kingdom-purposed friendship. What
do you have that God can use this way?

Whom Do You Fear?

*"I tell you, my friends, do not be afraid
of those who kill the body and after
that can do no more."*

LUKE 12:4 NIV

Whom do you fear? If it's anyone other
than God, take heart. You need not concern
yourself with anything that person can do
to you. Even those who can take your life
can't change your eternal destination. So if
someone doesn't like your faith, don't sweat
it. Put your trust in God and serve Him
faithfully, and you need not fear.

Never Alone

I am convinced that nothing can ever separate us from God's love. Neither death nor life, neither angels nor demons, neither our fears for today nor our worries about tomorrow—not even the powers of hell can separate us from God's love.

ROMANS 8:38 NLT

I read a poll that said being alone is one of women's worst fears. When we experience loss, we sometimes feel that we're struggling all alone; that others around us can't possibly comprehend the scope of our fears, our worries, our pain. But the Bible says we're not alone, that nothing can separate us from our heavenly Father. He is right there beside us, loving us, offering His companionship when we have none.

Disconnect from the World

*Whosoever therefore will be a friend
of the world is the enemy of God.*

JAMES 4:4 KJV

There are good friendships and bad ones.
When Christ becomes your best friend, other
relationships may become distant. Old, carnal
friendships no longer seem so attractive.
Your lifestyles clash, and old friends become
confused. But this separation is part of God's
plan of holiness. Jesus disconnects you
from the world and draws you close to His
people—Christian friends who share your
love for Him. Together you may reach out to
those old friends for Jesus, too.

Pure and Unspoiled

And everyone who has this hope fixed on Him purifies himself, just as He is pure.

1 JOHN 3:3 NASB

Don't you just love taking the first scoop of ice cream from a fresh half gallon? There's something about the smooth surface of unspoiled purity that satisfies the soul. It's the same with new jars of peanut butter, freshly fallen snow, or stretches of pristine, early morning beach sand. God looks at us that way—unblemished, pure and unspoiled—through our faith and hope in Him. Allow that thought to bring a smile to your face today.

Getting What You Give

Whoever sows sparingly will also reap sparingly, and whoever sows generously will also reap generously.

2 Corinthians 9:6 niv

What you give is what you get. That's true in life, and it's also true spiritually. Anyone who tries to hold finances close will be letting go of spiritual blessings, while the person who shares generously gains in so many ways. It's hard to give up worldly treasures, but when you give in the name of Jesus, you will never run short.

The Palm of His Hand

If I ride the wings of the morning, if I dwell by the farthest oceans, even there your hand will guide me, and your strength will support me.

PSALM 139:9–10 NLT

Surf foamed around my ankles as I lifted the burgundy starfish, its pointed tips curled in taut contraction. "It's okay, little fellow, I'll help you," I crooned, gently cradling the sea creature stranded by the outgoing tide. Tiny tentacles tickled my palm as the starfish relaxed, safe and protected. Likewise, God's hand rescues, supports, and guides us to life-sustaining waters when we're stranded. We're safe in the palm of His hand.

Turn to Him

*"I will be a Father to you, and you
shall be My sons and daughters,
says the LORD Almighty."*
2 CORINTHIANS 6:18 NKJV

Only unconfessed sin can separate you
from the Father. But God never desires such
distance. He wants to draw near, like a loving
Father who holds His child, provides for her,
and helps her at every turn.

Though your earthly father was less than
perfect, your heavenly Father is not. He heals
your hurts, solves your problems, and offers
His love at every turn. All you need to do is
turn to Him in love.

Cherished Desire

*God our Father loves us. He is kind and
has given us eternal comfort
and a wonderful hope.*

2 THESSALONIANS 2:16 CEV

Webster's definition of hope: "to cherish a
desire with expectation." In other words,
yearning for something wonderful you expect
to occur. Our hope in Christ is not just
yearning for something wonderful, as in "I
hope for a sunny beach day." It's a deep trust
with roots that extend from the beginning of
time to the infinite future. Our hope is not just
the anticipation of heaven, but the expectation
of a fulfilling life walking beside our Creator
and best Friend.

Nothing Is Hidden

*Nothing in all creation
is hidden from God's sight.*

HEBREWS 4:13 NIV

Good or bad, nothing escapes God's notice.
None of it is unknown to the Creator of the
universe. And because He knows all, we can
completely trust in God. He protects us from
the wicked and supports the good in our lives
because He knows just how both will touch
us. When sorrow or trouble comes our way,
we can count on His using it to benefit us—
here and in eternity.

First Love

But you must stay deeply rooted and firm in your faith. You must not give up the hope you received when you heard the good news.

COLOSSIANS 1:23 CEV

Do you remember the day you turned your life over to Christ? Can you recall the flood of joy and hope that coursed through your veins? Ah, the wonder of first love. Like romantic love that deepens and broadens with passing years, our relationship with Jesus evolves into a river of faith that endures the test of time.

He Is Faithful

*Blessed are those whose help is the
God of Jacob. . .the LORD. . .
he remains faithful forever.*
PSALM 146:5–6 NIV

You are not the only one who has experienced
God's faithfulness. Through the years,
believers have experienced His provision.
Read Old Testament accounts of those who
have never seen Him fail. Watch His acts in
the New Testament as He showed the church
that it could trust Him. God cannot fail His
children, and He will not fail you. Trust in the
God of Jacob, and pass on your testimony of
His faithfulness.

Astounding Rescue

Then I remember something that fills me with hope. The LORD's kindness never fails!

LAMENTATIONS 3:21–22 CEV

With our hectic lifestyles, pausing to remember the past isn't something we do very often. But perhaps we should. Then when doubts assault our faith, fears threaten to devour us, and disaster hovers like a dark cloud, we'll remember God's past loving-kindnesses. Hope will triumph over despair. Keeping a prayer journal is a wonderful way to chronicle answered prayer. We'll always remember the times when God's merciful hands rescued us in astounding ways.

DAY 92

All-Powerful

God is our refuge and strength,
an ever-present help in trouble.

PSALM 46:1 NIV

When we face serious troubles, people
often cannot provide the solution. Limited
by human frailty, even the most generous
of them can only help us so much. In every
trouble, we have a greater asset if we believe
in Jesus. Our all-powerful Creator offers
protection from harm and strength for the
longest trial. He always wants to come to our
aid. Facing a trouble of any size? Turn to Him
today.

Keeping Us in Stitches

The secret things belong to the LORD our God.
DEUTERONOMY 29:29 NIV

Have you ever noticed the messy underside
of a needlepoint picture? Ugly knots, loose
threads, and clashing colors appear random,
without pattern. Yet if you turn it over, an
exquisite, intricate design is revealed, each
stitch blending to create a beautiful finished
picture. Such is the fabric of our lives. The
knots and loose threads may not make sense
to us, but the Master Designer has a plan. The
secret design belongs to Him.

Never Forgotten

❦

*Who is like the LORD our God. . .who stoops
down to look on the heavens and the earth?*

PSALM 113:5–6 NIV

This all-powerful Lord, to whom the heavens
and earth are small, cares not just for your
universe, but for you. The verses that
follow these describe His love for even the
humblest person. Though you may face times
of struggle, your awesome Lord will never
forget you. One day, as verse 8 of this psalm
promises, even the humble can sit with
princes.

One Hunky Verse

*To Him who is able to do far more
abundantly beyond all that we ask or
think, according to the power that
works within us, to Him be the
glory. . .forever and ever. Amen.*

EPHESIANS 3:20–21 NASB

Don't you just love the bigness of this verse?
It radiates with the enormity of God—that
nothing is beyond His scope or power.
Read it aloud and savor the words *far more
abundantly.* Now repeat "beyond all that we
ask or think" three times, pondering each
word individually. Wow! If there was ever a
hunky verse to cast an attitude of gratitude
over our day, this is it. Yay, God!

Tender Love

*This is love: not that we loved God,
but that he loved us and sent his Son as
an atoning sacrifice for our sins.*

1 JOHN 4:10 NIV

We weren't sitting around thinking about
loving God before He touched our lives. God
began the process before we were even born.
He sent His Son to bring us into communion
with Him, and His Spirit drew us into a
relationship with Him. We respond to God's
overwhelmingly tender love when we invite
Jesus into our lives. Even so, many years of
obedience show our gratitude, but they never
repay His loving compassion.

A Lifetime Award

*O Lord, you alone are my hope.
I've trusted you, O LORD, from childhood.*
PSALM 71:5 NLT

My heart swelled like an over-inflated balloon. Tears blurred my vision as little Josh bounded for the stage, his blond cowlick flopping in the breeze. As his second grade Sunday school teacher, I had worked tirelessly to help him memorize ten Bible verses. Josh beamed at the shiny medal encircling his neck, but I knew that his true reward was God's Word implanted in his heart to guide him for the rest of his life.

Appreciation for Mercy

The LORD your God is a merciful God;
he will not abandon or destroy you.

DEUTERONOMY 4:31 NIV

Even when we fail God, He does not fail us.
He knows our frailty and has mercy when
we come to Him seeking forgiveness and
wanting to change our ways. Mercy never
holds grudges or seeks revenge, but it wants
the best for forgiven sinners. So our merciful
Lord calls us to make changes that show we
appreciate what He has done for us. Is some
appreciation called for in your life?

Permission to Mourn

*When I heard this, I sat down and cried.
Then for several days, I mourned;
I went without eating to show
my sorrow, and I prayed.*

NEHEMIAH 1:4 CEV

Bad news. When it arrives, what's your
reaction? Do you scream? Fall apart? Run
away? Nehemiah's response to bad news is a
model for us. First, he vented his sorrow. It's
okay to cry and mourn. Christians suffer pain
like everyone else—only we know the source
of inner healing. Disguising our struggle
doesn't make us look more spiritual. . .just
less real. Like Nehemiah, our next step is
to turn to the only true source of help and
comfort.

Joy in Our Troubles

Great is your love, reaching to the heavens; your faithfulness reaches to the skies.

Psalm 57:10 NIV

Has God's mercy touched your life so deeply that you wanted to shout His praises to the skies? That's how the psalmist felt as he trusted in God, despite his troubles. When we look to God in our troubles, our burdened hearts can still find joy. Though we are small and weak, He is most powerful. His strength will overcome our deepest problems if only we let it.

Pebbles

*"I will give you a new heart and put a new
spirit within you; and I will remove the
heart of stone from your flesh and
give you a heart of flesh."*

EZEKIEL 36:26 NASB

So many things can harden our hearts: overwhelming loss; shattered dreams; even scar
tissue from broken hearts, disillusionment,
and disappointment. To avoid pain, we simply
turn off feelings. Our hearts become petrified
rock—heavy, cold, and rigid. But God can crack
our hearts of stone from the inside out and replace that miserable pile of pebbles with soft,
feeling hearts of flesh. The amazing result is a
brand-new, hope-filled spirit.

Overflowing Mercy

❦

Israel, put your hope in the LORD,
for with the LORD is unfailing love
and with him is full redemption.

PSALM 130:7 NIV

Why hope in God, even in dire situations?
Because every one of His people greatly needs
His overflowing mercy. Our lives are frail, but
He is not. Jesus brings the redemption we
require. No matter what we face, Jesus walks
with us. We need only trust faithfully that His
salvation is on the way.

Do a Little Dance

Then Miriam. . .took a tambourine and led all the women as they played their tambourines and danced.

EXODUS 15:20 NLT

Can you imagine the enormous celebration that broke out among the children of Israel when God miraculously saved them from Pharaoh's army? Even dignified prophetess Miriam grabbed her tambourine and cut loose with her girlfriends. Despite adverse circumstances, she heard God's music and did His dance. Isn't that our goal today? To Hear God's music above the world's cacophony and do His dance as we recognize everyday miracles in our lives?

Trust God

❧

Abraham answered, "God himself will provide the lamb for the burnt offering, my son."

GENESIS 22:8 NIV

Though God had commanded Abraham to sacrifice his son Isaac, the patriarch had faith his son would not die. All it took was a ram caught in a bush. Because of Abraham's faith, the sheep was just where he needed it at the right moment. God provided just what was necessary—a sacrifice and a living son. Do you need God's provision today? Trust the God who made a way for Abraham to make a way for you, too.

Payday

❦

*"Go into all the world
and preach the gospel to all creation."*
MARK 16:15 NASB

One day as our family discussed the Great
Commission over dinner, my salesman
husband asked my young daughter if she knew
what commission meant. "Sure," she replied.
"It's what you get paid at the end for what you
did in the beginning."

Our commission will be paid in heaven
when we're surrounded not only by dear
friends and family with whom we shared our
faith, but also the souls reached by missions
we supported with our time, money, and
energies.

Let His Light Shine

❦

For Christ's sake, I delight in weaknesses,
in insults, in hardships, in persecutions,
in difficulties. For when I am weak,
then I am strong.

2 CORINTHIANS 12:10 NIV

Only God can make you strong in the weak places. In those spots of persecution and hardship, His power and grace shine through your fragile vessel as you live as a faithful Christian. When you feel broken and useless, trust in Him to fill your flaws, and His light will shine through the cracks of your pain and reach a hurting world.

Soul Sister

"I always see the Lord near me, and I will not be afraid with him at my right side. Because of this, my heart will be glad, my words will be joyful, and I will live in hope."

ACTS 2:25–26 CEV

Laughter is the soul sister of joy; they often travel together. Humor is the primary catalyst for releasing joy into our souls and making our hearts glad. It's healthy for us, too! Laughter is cleansing and healing, a powerful salve for the wounds of life. . .a natural medicine and tremendous stress reliever. Laughing is to joy what a 50 percent off sign is to shopping. It motivates us to seek more, more, more!

Safe in His Will

*Your hand will guide me,
your right hand will hold me fast.*

PSALM 139:10 NIV

Need to make a life-changing decision?
God wants to be part of it. As the psalmist
understood, allowing Him to guide your steps
means you won't get off track and land in
a nasty situation. For the believer, the best
place to be is in the palm of God's hand, safe
from harm and in the center of His will.

JOY: Jesus Occupying You

May all who fear you find in me a cause for joy, for I have put my hope in your word.

PSALM 119:74 NLT

Have you ever met someone you immediately knew was filled with joy? The kind of effervescent joy that bubbles up and overflows, covering everyone around her with warmth and love and acceptance. We love to be near people filled with Jesus-joy. And even more, as Christians we want to be like them! Lord, remind us how.

Every Step of the Way

❧

He will be our guide even to the end.
PSALM 48:14 NIV

———————————

When we are facing dire troubles, God never deserts us. As life ebbs away, He does not step back from our need. No, the Eternal One guides us every step of the way, whether life is joyous or discouraging. God never gives up on you and never fails you. So don't give up on yourself. When times are hard, grab onto Him more firmly. He will never leave you nor forsake you. And in the end, you will step into His arms in heaven.

As the Tide Turns

"He will not falter or be discouraged till he establishes justice on earth. In his teaching the islands will put their hope."

ISAIAH 42:4 NIV

Change. . .besides our unalterable Lord, it's the only thing constant in this world. Yet the only person who likes change is a baby with a wet diaper. Isaiah prophesied that the Almighty will one day create positive change on earth. Like the tides that clean beach debris after a storm, positive change washes away the old and refreshes with the new. In this we hope.

You Can't Go Wrong

"In your unfailing love you will lead the people you have redeemed. In your strength you will guide them to your holy dwelling."

EXODUS 15:13 NIV

By following Jesus, you always head in the right direction. Though the way may seem dark or convoluted and you may often wonder if you're on the right track, as His Spirit leads you, you cannot go wrong. Your powerful Lord directs you in His everlasting way. If you start to go wrong, He will guide your steps. God's love never deserts His obedient child.

Up Is the Only Out

Let them lie face down in the dust,
for there may be hope at last.

LAMENTATIONS 3:29 NLT

The Old Testament custom for grieving people was to lie prostrate and cover themselves with ashes. Perhaps the thought was that when you're wallowing in the dust, at least you can't descend any further. There's an element of hope in knowing that there's only one way to go: up. If a recent loss has you sprawled in the dust, know that God doesn't waste pain in our lives. He will use it for some redeeming purpose.

Unfailing Love

*The Lord delights in those who. . .
put their hope in his unfailing love.*

PSALM 147:11 NIV

We can hope in a lot of things that fail us
miserably, or we can enjoy a blind optimism
that leads us into trouble. But when we hope
in God, who has loved us completely, our
faith cannot fail. Could the One who delights
in our trust forget to bless our anticipation of
an eternity with Him?

Make God joyful today as you put your
trust in His everlasting love.

Welcome Back

Train up a child in the way he should go:
and when he is old, he will not depart from it.
PROVERBS 22:6 KJV

I'll never forget the tender bedtime family
gatherings on my sister's bed when I was a
child. After reading a Bible story from the big
picture Bible, we took turns praying. When I
had children, I established the same tradition
in our home. The Bible promises that if we
instill God's Word and principles in our
children, they will one day return to it. It may
take time, but God's Word will not return
void.

Prosperity Returns

*"Then I will make up to you for the years
that the swarming locust has eaten."*

JOEL 2:25 NASB

Those of us who rejoice in God can trust that
even though the consuming locusts of life
destroy our blessings, God will replace them.
Though hardship makes us struggle awhile,
God turns the situation around and pours out
blessings on His faithful people. Prosperity
returns to those who love Him well. In
heaven or on earth, the blessing appears
again.

Time Out for Encouragement

*Do all that is in your heart,
for the LORD is with you.*

2 SAMUEL 7:3 NKJV

Every day, why not encourage yourself? Take a few moments to fill your thoughts with gentle words of assurance and affirmation. Reflect on God's many kindnesses toward you in the past, and visualize the good plans He has for you right now. If you're lacking energy or feeling unappreciated, let Him whisper words of assurance in your heart. No, it's not just a trick to get yourself pumped for the duties of the day, but the way God renews a tired spirit, boosts sagging confidence, heightens appreciation for the present hour, and restores genuine enthusiasm.

Praise God—
No Matter What

The king will rejoice in God;
all who swear by God will glory in him.
PSALM 63:11 NIV

Need some joy in your life? Start praising
God, and no matter what messy situations
you face today, you'll begin rejoicing. Praise
Him for who He is—His immense, loving
nature that has blessed you so much. Thank
Him for the love He's showered on you. As
you remember His love, sorrow loses its grasp
on your life.

Rocky Road

For through the Spirit we eagerly await by faith the righteousness for which we hope.
GALATIANS 5:5 NIV

My daughter's five-pound Russian Terror (oops—that's Terrier) is anything but righteous. Rocky dashes after cars, nibbles poisonous plants, and routinely ingests ripped-apart rugs. In order to guide said pup along the path of righteousness, doors must close. Our paths of righteousness are also guided by the One who shuts doors according to what's best for us. So, girlfriends—enough howling, whining, and scratching at closed doors!

God Is Great

I know that the LORD is great,
that our Lord is greater than all gods.

PSALM 135:5 NIV

Other "gods" contend with Jesus in the marketplace of ideas, and devout Christians may encounter contention. But just as the psalmist recognized God's greatness, we can, too, as we look at the world around us. No other would-be deity shows forth its glory in creation. No other has provided God's gracious salvation. If our Lord controls our lives, how can we look to any other gods?

Not Suzie Homemaker

*The Spirit has given each of us
a special way of serving others.*

1 CORINTHIANS 12:7 CEV

My friend Denise has the gift of hospitality.
She welcomes people into her home and
makes them feel loved through her thoughtful
accents: serving food on her best china,
lighting scented candles, offering cozy
furnishings. Hospitality is not my gift. My
guests get bagged chips, flat soda, and leave
coated in cat hair. God taught me not to
compare and despair, for He has given each
of us our own gift to be used for His service.
What's yours?

Live Devotedly

*Do you not know that you are the temple
of God and that the Spirit of
God dwells in you?*

1 CORINTHIANS 3:16 NKJV

God lives within you, not in a distant place.
When you act according to His Word, He
acts. When you fail, people may begin to
doubt Him. That's why Paul encourages you
to live devotedly for your Lord. As one of His
people, you're filled with His potent Spirit,
who empowers you to live a holy life. Live in
His strength always.

Working Out

I will never give up hope or stop praising you.
PSALM 71:14 CEV

Praise is like a muscle; if we don't exercise
it regularly, it becomes weak and atrophied.
But if we flex and extend an attitude of
gratitude daily, praise grows into a strong,
dependable force that nurtures hope and
carries us through the worst of circumstances.
Like Helen Keller, though blind and deaf,
we'll praise our Creator: "I thank God for my
handicaps, for through them, I have found
myself, my work, and my God."

Love Is Action

Dear friends, let us love one another, for love comes from God. Everyone who loves has been born of God and knows God.

1 JOHN 4:7 NIV

Want to see love? Look at God. Seeking love in this world is bound to be confusing. But in our Lord, we see the clean, clear lines of real love—love we can share with our families, friends, and fellow believers. Love for our enemies. Love for our Savior. Apart from God, we cannot truly and sacrificially love others. Love isn't just a feeling, but the actions we take as we follow Him.

Inexplicable Strength

"*The joy of the LORD is your strength.*"
NEHEMIAH 8:10 NASB

Joy is not based on the circumstances around
us. It is not synonymous with happiness. God
promised believers His deep, abiding joy—
not fleeting happiness, which is here today,
gone tomorrow. The joy of the Lord rises
above external situations and supernaturally
overshadows everything else to become our
inexplicable, internal strength.

Seeing God

❧⚬⚬⚬❧

No one has seen God at any time.
If we love one another, God abides in us,
and His love has been perfected in us.

1 JOHN 4:12 NKJV

How do we see God? Often, it's through
other people. That's why it's important to
have a compassionate Christian witness—
people see you and think God is like you if
you claim His name. In that way, many people
have gotten erroneous concepts about the
Savior. But many more have come to love
Him through faithful testimonies. Today you
can love others and show them clearly what
Jesus looks like.

Forever Joy

We don't look at the troubles we can see now. . . . For the things we see now will soon be gone, but the things we cannot see will last forever.

2 Corinthians 4:18 nlt

A painter's first brush strokes look like random blobs—no discernable shape, substance, or clue as to what the completed painting will be. But in time, the skilled artist brings order to perceived chaos. Initial confusion is forgotten in joyful admiration of the finished masterpiece.

We often can't see past the blobs of trouble on our life canvases. We must trust that the Artist has a masterpiece underway. And there will be great joy in its completion.

Life-Altering Impact

*We were therefore buried with him
through baptism into death in order that,
just as Christ was raised from the dead
through the glory of the Father,
we too may live a new life.*

ROMANS 6:4 NIV

Baptism is a picture of the old, sinful nature's
death and the new faith life God gives those
who trust in Him. Belief in Jesus has a life-
altering impact. One moment a sinful person
is dead, held in sin's grasp. The next she
becomes an entirely new person, alive in
her Savior. Only Jesus offers this glorious
freedom. Has He given it to you?

Perfect Love

*Love never gives up, never loses faith,
is always hopeful, and endures
through every circumstance.*

1 CORINTHIANS 13:7 NLT

We have relationships in three directions:
upward (with God), outward (with others),
and inward (with ourselves). We are bound
to be disappointed at one time or another by
the latter two. Because of human frailty, we
will inevitably experience failure by others
and even ourselves. Our imperfect love will be
strained to the breaking point. But our Creator
will never fail us—His perfect love never gives
up on us.

Living in the Light

*In him was life,
and that life was the light of all mankind.*
JOHN 1:4 NIV

Jesus is a Christian's life and light, as anyone
who has walked with Him for a while can tell
you. Everything is different once He enters
a soul. As a result, the new believer begins
to make changes, cleaning out the dark
corners of her existence so that the bright
light shining within her will not fall on dirty
places. She's living in the light, following
Jesus.

Three Little Words

*Three things will last
forever—faith, hope, and love.*
1 CORINTHIANS 13:13 NLT

Don't you get tired of throwing away panty hose? It's hard to believe that modern technology can scan quivers inside our livers and detect nickel-sized puddles on Mars, but we still can't manufacture hose that won't run. Yep, there are precious few things that endure. Only three, the Bible says: faith, hope, and love. Three things that will never break down, wear out, or get lost. These are the only things worth keeping.

You Are Valuable

Who can find a virtuous woman?
for her price is far above rubies.
PROVERBS 31:10 KJV

Are you a virtuous woman? If so, you are truly valuable, no matter how unbelievers criticize you. Proverbs 31 says you can have a profitable life with good relationships, a happy home life, and successful business ventures if you run your life according to God's principles. So don't worry about the opinions of others if they don't mesh with God's. Instead, obey Him and be a valuable jewel to your Lord.

New Life

*God is so good, and by raising Jesus
from death, he has given us new life
and a hope that lives on.*

1 PETER 1:3 CEV

The words of a song I wrote while pregnant
with my first child exult in the similarities
between new physical life and fresh spiritual
life in Christ: "New life stirs within me now.
Like a soft breeze, transforming me now. It's a
miracle of love, precious blessing from above.
My heart has taken wings. . .lift me up!"

New life. By the goodness of God, we can
experience this precious transformation no less
miraculous than a baby growing within us.

Love and Obey

"Whoever has my commands and keeps them is the one who loves me."

JOHN 14:21 NIV

Do you feel you love God with all your heart? Then show it by obeying Him. Jesus paved the path for you. Through His own sacrificial life, He showed you what it means to obey the Father. A Christian who lives for herself, rather than God, shows wavering commitment. One who loves God wholeheartedly walks in Jesus' way, obeying His commands in scripture. Here is where we start: Love God? Then obey Him, too.

Time-out

"The LORD will not abandon His people."
1 SAMUEL 12:22 NASB

Do you remember when, as a little girl, you languished alone in your room as punishment? Or maybe you sat with your nose plastered to the corner in time-out. It felt like your parents had abandoned you, didn't it? As adults, we sometimes feel abandoned when that's not the case at all. We're actually in a place strategically chosen by a loving Father to teach us, broaden us, and improve us in the end.

DAY 136

Blessings Will Come

*"All these blessings shall come upon you
and overtake you, because you obey
the voice of the LORD your God."*

DEUTERONOMY 28:2 NKJV

Obey God; receive blessings. It seems simple
enough, doesn't it? Then why do we obey and
only get in more trouble than before? Perhaps
it's because we're looking at it from our
perspective, not His. Blessings do not always
follow on the heels of obedience; they often
take time to appear. Today's blessings may
result from long-ago faithfulness. But because
God has promised, we know good things
come if only we wait.

Bigger and Better

*Waiting does not diminish us, any more
than waiting diminishes a pregnant
mother. . . . The longer we wait. . .
the more joyful our expectancy.*

ROMANS 8:24–25 MSG

———————————

Life is filled with waiting—on slow people,
transportation, doctor reports, even for God
to act. Waiting often requires patience we
don't have. It feels like perpetual pregnancy—
anticipating a baby that is never delivered.
The secret is to clasp hands with our Lord.
He offers His shield of protection from
impatience, irritability, and anger and replaces
them with self-control, kindness, and joy.
Waiting is inevitable, but we can draw closer
to the Father in the waiting.

DAY 138

Into Eternity

❦

Blessed are they that do his commandments,
that they may have right to the tree
of life, and may enter in through
the gates into the city.

REVELATION 22:14 KJV

———————————

The blessings of obedience not only impact us
today; they follow us into eternity. Whatever
we do to please God never dies. By trusting
in Jesus, the works that demonstrate our
faith give us joy now and remain secure for
the future in the One who never changes.
We look forward to life in the New Jerusalem
even as we reap His blessings now.

Please Rescue Me

I long for you to rescue me!
Your word is my only hope.
PSALM 119:81 CEV

Have you ever longed to be rescued?
Stranded after shredding knee ligaments
during a remote mountain skiing accident, I
waited helplessly for rescuers to arrive. All
alone on the raw Canadian mountainside, I felt
fear mount. Freezing temperatures, prowling
cougars, and unrelenting pain threatened to
engulf me in despair. So I did the most and the
least I could do: I prayed and recited scripture.
And my faithful heavenly Father rescued me
with His peace.

God Hears

"Therefore I tell you, whatever you ask for in prayer, believe that you have received it, and it will be yours."

MARK 11:24 NIV

This verse is not prescribing some magical incantation, but faith that God hears and answers our requests. When we trust that He knows our needs and wants to respond to them, we are in a position to receive. Would Jesus be proud of our requests? Do we seek the good of others? Or do we look only to our own desires? God answers prayers that reflect His will. How do yours stack up against this measure?

Hope Resurrected

We had hoped that he would be the one to set Israel free! But it has already been three days since all this happened.

LUKE 24:21 CEV

The scenario for this scripture is quite unusual. Two of Jesus' disciples are describing their lost hope due to the events surrounding Jesus' death to none other than Jesus Himself. They don't recognize Him as they walk together on the road to Emmaus after His resurrection. Spiritual cataracts blind them to the hope they thought was dead—right in front of them! Let's open our spiritual eyes to Jesus, who is walking beside us.

Love Your Enemy

*"But I tell you, love your enemies
and pray for those who persecute you."*

MATTHEW 5:44 NIV

Without God's strength, could any of us
follow this command of Jesus for more than
a very brief time? Consistently loving an
enemy is a real challenge. If you hurt from
pain inflicted by another, you hardly want to
pray for her. But loving actions and prayer can
bring great peace between two people at odds
with each other. For those who consistently
follow this command, strife may not last
forever.

Sprung

I will free your prisoners from death in a waterless dungeon. Come back to the place of safety, all you prisoners who still have hope!

ZECHARIAH 9:11–12 NLT

In the marvelous book, *The Count of Monte Cristo*, Edmond Dantes is unjustly imprisoned. Against all odds, God enables him to escape and eventually return victorious, a hope-filled man.

Have you ever felt trapped in a prison of hopelessness? Financial difficulties, poor health, unemployment, rocky marriage, delinquent children—there are countless dungeons that shackle us. But God promises hope and freedom from our prisons. Jesus bailed us out!

Healing Power

The prayer of faith will save the sick, and the Lord will raise him up. And if he has committed sins, he will be forgiven.

JAMES 5:15 NKJV

Have you seen the amazing healing power of prayer? As faithful Christians lift a sufferer up to God, He works in the body, but also in the heart and soul. Know someone who is ill? Pray for physical health to return. But don't forget to include spiritual needs, for the Great Physician treats the whole person. Some spiritual issue may be the real problem that requires healing.

Power Source

*He gives strength to the weary
and increases the power of the weak.*

ISAIAH 40:29 NIV

Sometimes we feel as if our backs will break under the burdens we carry: debt, responsibilities, impossible schedules. But our God promises to strengthen and empower us if we turn to Him for help. He knows. He cares. He is able.

It's been written that persecuted European Christians don't pray for God to lessen their loads like American Christians do. Instead, they pray for stronger backs.

Prayer from the Heart

Some trust in chariots, and some in horses;
but we will remember the name
of the LORD our God.

PSALM 20:7 NKJV

This may seem an odd prayer for a king going out to battle, but it shows where David's heart was. He knew his war equipment could fail, but God could not.

What danger can we face that God is incapable of defending us from? None. Where have we placed our trust—in Him or in worldly defenses?

No Call-Waiting

*"Call on me and come and pray to me,
and I will listen to you."*

JEREMIAH 29:12 NIV

"I will listen to you." Every woman's dream.
   Jeremiah knew the importance of being
listened to. He proclaimed God's message
for forty years to the unseeing, unhearing,
unresponsive nation of Judah. His ironic good
news: God is listening!
   Do you ever feel like no one's listening?
The Bible says God hears us every time we
utter His name. How precious we are to our
Creator that He bends His omnipotent ear
each time we call on Him.

Overcoming the Sin Barrier

Godly sorrow brings repentance that leads to salvation and leaves no regret.

2 CORINTHIANS 7:10 NIV

Godly sorrow comes when we feel the pain of our own sins. As we recognize our own wrongdoing and know that our actions have hurt us, others, and even the heart of God, we reach the place to do something about it. We repent, and God offers His salvation.

Has sin come between you and your Savior? Turn at once in sorrow and ask Him to make everything right in your heart and soul. You'll never be sorry you did.

Juiced

God is our refuge and strength,
a very present help in trouble.

PSALM 46:1 NASB

Remember the scene from the movie *Air Force One*, when Harrison Ford, as the U.S. President, calls for help from the belly of a terrorist-hijacked plane after much death-defying effort? Just as the crucial call is dialed, his cell phone battery conks out. Can you identify? What a relief that our direct line to God—prayer—is always juiced and never needs recharging!

Cleansing Spirit

*I came not to call the righteous,
but sinners to repentance.*
LUKE 5:32 KJV

Repentance isn't meant for "good people"
who only have "tiny" sins to confess. This
verse reminds us that no sin is too awful for
God to hear about it. God calls all who are
sinful—those who most need Him and have
the most to fear from His awesome holiness.
Each of us may hesitate to confess sins and
admit to wrongs that embarrass us. But we
are just the ones He calls. One moment of
repentance and His Spirit cleanses our lives.

Slip-Sliding Away

Instruct those who are rich. . .not to
be conceited or to fix their hope on the
uncertainty of riches, but on God,
who richly supplies us with
all things to enjoy.

1 TIMOTHY 6:17 NASB

My friend Claire lived large with a millionaire husband, enormous house, designer clothes, and flashy convertible—even a cook (to my envy!). But suddenly the economy headed south, and in the twinkle of a bank vault key, she lost it all. Divorced, homeless, and bitter, Claire was forced to wait tables to pay her ill son's medical bills. We can't depend on money—here today, gone tomorrow. Our hope must be fixed on our eternal God.

Compassion to Others

"And if he sins against you seven times in a day, and seven times in a day returns to you, saying, 'I repent,' you shall forgive him."

LUKE 17:4 NKJV

When another offends us, do we pass on the forgiveness we have received? That's what Jesus commanded. Remembering how gracious God has been to us, we need to show it to those who affront us, too. As we think of our many sins that God put behind His back, can we fail to show compassion to others?

Daily Duties

Let all that you do be done in love.

1 CORINTHIANS 16:14 NASB

Sometimes we get so wrapped up in our daily
to-do lists that we put our duties above people.
"Leave me alone until this project is finished,
kids." "Sorry, Sue, I'm too busy to have lunch."
"Oh, I don't have time to talk to Mom today; I'll
let the answering machine get it."

How, then, can we ever share the love of
Christ with those we've shoved out of our
way? People don't care how much you know
until they know how much you care.

Available 24/7

*"Blessed is the man to whom
the Lord shall not impute sin."*

ROMANS 4:8 NKJV

Sin forgiven: What a wonderful thought!
No longer do we need to be dragged into
wrongdoing, because God has cleansed our
hearts. His Spirit sweeps through us, lifting
the burden of sin from our lives. Though we
still fail, in Christ, God will not hold the sin
against us. Forgiveness, available 24/7, sends
His Spirit through our lives again and again.

One Nation under God

The poor are filled with hope,
and injustice is silenced.
JOB 5:16 CEV

"Give me your tired, your poor, your huddled
masses. . . ." beckons the Statue of Liberty,
offering a home and freedom to hurting
people. Many of our ancestors flocked to
American shores that were offering freedom
of worship and an end to the injustice of
religious persecution. May we never forget
the sacrifices they made to pursue the hope of
providing their children—you and me—with
a nation founded on Christian principles.
Let's strive to preserve that hope for future
generations.

DAY 156

Reconcilers

God was reconciling the world to himself in Christ, not counting people's sins against them. And he has committed to us the message of reconciliation.

2 CORINTHIANS 5:19 NIV

The Lord loved you so much that He paid a huge price to draw you into His arms. Jesus' sacrifice destroyed the sin barrier that separates humanity and God. Those who repent are reconciled to their holy God. But faith does not stop there. He makes us reconcilers, too, as He sends us out with the message that has meant so much: "God loves you, too."

A Strong Tower

The name of the Lord is a fortified tower;
the righteous run to it and are safe.
PROVERBS 18:10 NIV

We of the twenty-first century tend to limit
our references to God, but ancient Hebrew
translations offer a broader perspective. There
is intrinsic hope in the names of God: Elohim
(Mighty Creator), El Olam (The Everlasting
God), Yahweh Yireh (The Lord Will Provide),
Yahweh Shalom (The Lord Is Peace), Yawheh
Tsuri (The Lord, My Rock), and Abba (Father)
to name a few. Let's broaden our scope of His
powerful name in our prayers today.

Saving Grace

❧❦❧

My soul finds rest in God;
my salvation comes from him.

PSALM 62:1 NIV

_____

At the moment you repented of your sins and
asked Jesus to control your life, God saved
you. But He didn't stop there. Each day of
your life, He continues His saving work. He
redirects you, protects you, and provides for
your every need. In any trouble, rest in Him.
He will not fail.

24/7

He will not let your foot slip—he who watches over you will not slumber.
Psalm 121:3 NIV

I love hiking the winding mountain paths near our remote Smoky Mountain cabin. Sometimes I get so caught up in watching hummingbirds or admiring cliff-side vistas that I stumble, forgetting that inattention could be deadly. How comforting to know that our Lord is always alert as He watches over us. We don't have to worry that an important prayer will slip by while He sneezes or that He'll nap through our surgery. He's always on duty.

Shine for Him

❧◆❧◆❧

*[Jesus] gave himself for us to redeem us
from all wickedness and to purify for
himself a people that are his very own,
eager to do what is good.*

TITUS 2:14 NIV

Is there any sin from which Jesus cannot save
us? No. As long as we look to Him, He will
lead us into increasing, joyous holiness.

God takes sinful people and changes
their lives, making them His hands in an evil
world. As His people draw near Him, putting
off sin, their good works shine forth the
nature of their Savior. Will you shine for Him
today?

One Gutsy Gal

*"It could be that you were made queen
for a time like this!"*
ESTHER 4:14 CEV

Crowned queen after winning a beauty
contest, Esther was only allowed audience
with her king when summoned. A wave of his
scepter would pardon her from execution, but
he was a hard man—and unpredictable. When
Esther learned of a plot to destroy her people,
she faced a tough decision. She was the only
one who could save them—at supreme risk.
God had intentionally placed her in that
position for that time. What's your divinely
ordained position?

Our Partner

Continue to work out your salvation
with fear and trembling.

PHILIPPIANS 2:12 NIV

Salvation is hard work! Not only did it require
Jesus' crucifixion for our sins, but we have a
part in the effort, too. We have to live out the
commands in God's Word that make our faith
have an impact on our world. But we need
not feel discouraged, for we are not alone in
the labor. God acts through us, by His Spirit.
What better working partner could we have
than God Himself?

Cool Summer Shower

*He will renew your life
and sustain you in your old age.*
RUTH 4:15 NIV

Ruth's blessing of renewal is applicable to
us today. Renovatio is Latin for "rebirth."
It means casting off the old and embracing
the new: a revival of spirit, a renovation of
attitude. Something essential for women to
espouse every day of their lives. Like a cool
rain shower on a sizzling summer day, Ruth's
hope was renewed by her Lord's touch, and
ours will be, too, if we look to Him for daily
replenishing.

Spiritual Training

All Scripture. . .is useful for. . .training in righteousness, so that the servant of God may be thoroughly equipped for every good work.

2 TIMOTHY 3:16–17 NIV

Did you realize that God prepares you to do good works every day of your life? Because you believe in Him, He will lead you to do good, following His plan for your life.

How do you start? By reading the scriptures, His guidebook. There you will learn what to believe, how to act, and how to speak with love. Soon you'll be ready to put into action all you've learned.

Zombie Zone

❧❦❧

Be joyful in hope,
patient in affliction, faithful in prayer.
ROMANS 12:12 NIV

———————

Affliction has a tendency to suck the joy right out of our lives, leaving us stranded in the dully-funks. You know—that black hole of existence where our minds fog, emotions go numb, eyes glaze over, and we languish in a state of spiritual dullness. A spiritual zombie zone. But if we're faithful in prayer, God will be faithful to rescue us from those joy-sucking dully-funks and fill us to the brim with His abundant joy.

Serving Others

*You. . .were called to be free. But do not use
your freedom to indulge the flesh; rather,
serve one another humbly in love.*

GALATIANS 5:13 NIV

As women, we know a lot about serving: we
serve on many fronts and sometimes wonder
why this is our lot. God tells us He freed us
from sin, not to do what we like but so we
can share His love. If we're tempted to fulfill
our own sinful desires, let's remind ourselves
why we are here—we obey Jesus by doing
good for others. If that's not our goal, we
need redirection from Him.

Laughter and Hope

A joyful heart is good medicine.
PROVERBS 17:22 NASB

Laughter is to hope as nonstick cooking spray is to a shiny new muffin tin: it keeps the goo from sticking. Once the batter of everyday responsibility hardens and adheres to our attitudes, it's awfully hard to scrape off enough crust for hope to shine through. But if we coat our day with a little laughter and the joy of the Lord, problems will slide off a lot better. And hope sparkles.

You're Equipped

In Christ you have been brought to fullness.
He is the head over every power
and authority.

COLOSSIANS 2:10 NIV

Do you feel incomplete or inadequate, unable
to carry out the tasks God has given you?
You aren't, you know, if you tap into His
Spirit. God equips you to do all things in
Him. If you feel overwhelmed, make sure you
haven't taken on tasks rightfully belonging to
someone else. God does not overload your life
with busyness. He has a purpose for all you
do. So be certain you're serving in the right
place, doing the work He planned for you.

Two-Stranded Rope

*The widow who is really in need and left
all alone puts her hope in God and
continues night and day to pray
and to ask God for help.*

1 TIMOTHY 5:5 NIV

Some women feel as though they are
irreparably weakened when they are widowed.
Where there once were three strands of a
sturdy rope (his, hers, and God's), there now
are two. But those who persevere through
faith and true grit say the secret is to learn to
rejoice in what's left instead of lamenting what
has been lost. Look forward. Move forward.
Keep that two-stranded rope strong, and never
lose hope of a better tomorrow.

Grace Is a Gift

*But unto every one of us is given grace
according to the measure of
the gift of Christ.*

<small>EPHESIANS 4:7 KJV</small>

We don't usually think of grace as a "spiritual
gift." But consider: it's the basis for all the
gifts God gives us. Without His gracious
forgiveness, we'd have nothing spiritually.
Our sins so separate us, that only His
forgiveness allows us to approach Him.
Whether we receive a large measure of grace
or a smaller one, it is the perfect gift, given by
Jesus, just for us. Let's appreciate what it cost
Him and walk in Him today.

Bet the Farm

Whoever plows and threshes should be
able to do so in the hope of sharing
in the harvest.

1 CORINTHIANS 9:10 NIV

———————————

There's a young man who works in children's
church with me who is loud, brash, impulsive,
an incessant talker, and loves the Lord with all
his heart. The kids think he's hilarious. I think
he's obnoxious. But I must remind myself that
God uses him in unique ways to reach young
hearts with the gospel that I never could. He's
a plowman and I'm a thresher, and we work
together to harvest souls into God's kingdom.

For His Glory

We have different gifts, according to the grace given to each of us.

ROMANS 12:6 NIV

Your spiritual gifts are tailored especially for you. God has a purpose for your life. To help you accomplish it, He has given just the gifts you need—nothing more, nothing less. Doesn't knowing that God has gifted you in just the right way make you feel special? Thank Him for those gifts today, and use them for the glory of His kingdom and to help others.

The Salvage Master

❧

We are pressed on every side by troubles,
but we are not crushed.

2 CORINTHIANS 4:8 NLT

Many women struggle with depression
at some point in their lives: post-partum,
kids-partum (empty nest), brain-partum
(menopause), and anytime in between. We feel
that we are being compressed into a rock-hard
cube like the product of a trash compactor.
The normal details of life suddenly become
perplexing and overwhelming. But God does
not abandon us to the garbage dump. He is the
Salvage Master and recycles us into sterling
images of His glory.

Reach Out

*Try to excel in [gifts] that
build up the church.*

1 CORINTHIANS 14:12 NIV

Paul's words to the Corinthians were meant
for us, too. We should build up the church,
not ourselves, through our spiritual gifts.
When God gave you a special combination
of spiritual abilities, it wasn't to make you
feel important. He designed them to help you
reach out to those who need to accept Him as
Savior and to support believers who also have
your mission to reach the world. Is that how
you're using your gifts today?

Look to the Sunrise

I rise before dawn and cry for help;
I have put my hope in your word.
PSALM 119:147 NIV

Could be stress or worry or berserk hormones.
Whatever the cause, many women find
themselves staring at their dark bedroom
ceilings in the wee morning hours. We try
counting sheep, but they morph into naughty
little children, and we exhaust ourselves
chasing them through fitful dreams. We're
tormented by the "what if's," guilted by the
"should have's," and jolted wider awake by the
"don't forget to's." But a new day is dawning,
and help is but a prayer away.

Christian Strength

*Finally, be strong in the Lord
and in his mighty power.*
EPHESIANS 6:10 NIV

When you rely on God's strength, what are
you tapping into? Not some small pool of
power that fails at a critical moment. The
Christian's strength is mighty because God
is mighty. He who created the universe does
not have a short arm that cannot reach down
to your situation. Shining stars testify to His
authority. Galaxies in space are ordered by
His hand. He can order your life, too. Ask
Him to use His strength in your life, and you
will have all you need.

Chill

I lie awake thinking of you, meditating on you through the night. Because you are my helper, I sing for joy in the shadow of your wings.

PSALM 63:6–7 NLT

Are you a worrier? Do you frequently find yourself working up a sweat building molehills into mountains during the midnight hours? This passage suggests an alternative for that nasty and unproductive habit. Instead of worrying, try meditating on the loving-kindness of God. Like a distressed chick tucked safely beneath the snug wings of the mother hen, allow the joy of being loved and protected to relax your tense muscles and ease you into peaceful rest.

DAY 178

Have Courage

Be on your guard; stand firm in the faith;
be courageous; be strong.
1 Corinthians 16:13 niv

Being a Christian can take lots of courage. As
the world around us becomes increasingly
hostile to God and our personal lives
become tense because of our beliefs, we feel
the challenge. But we are not defenseless.
Christians through the ages have faced these
troubles and triumphed. The Lord who
supported them gives us strength, too. Let
us stand fast for Jesus, calling on His Spirit
to strengthen our lives. Then we will be
strong indeed.

Showers of Blessing

Do the skies themselves send down showers?
No, it is you, LORD our God. Therefore
our hope is in you, for you are
the one who does all this.

JEREMIAH 14:22 NIV

Have you ever stood in your parched garden, praying for rain? The plants you've nurtured from seeds are wilting, flower petals litter the ground, fruit withers on the vine. Then thunder clouds roll and the skies burst forth with reinvigorating rain.

There will be dry times, too, in our spiritual gardens, but our hope is in the Lord our God, who sends showers to revive us. Deluge us today, Lord.

Uplift Others

❧❧❧❧

*We who are strong ought to bear with
the failings of the weak and not
to please ourselves.*

ROMANS 15:1 NIV

So God has made you strong in some area—
perhaps by experience, as you have struggled
to obey Him. Now, how do you respond
to others? Don't criticize those who have
different experiences or other strengths,
or carp about the failings of new, weak
Christians. Instead, use your power to uplift
others. Come alongside and help. Then God's
strength will have helped you both.

Snippets of Hope

*I also pray that you will understand
the incredible greatness of God's
power for us who believe him.*

EPHESIANS 1:19 NLT

Daydreams are snippets of hope for our souls.
Yearnings for something better, something
more exciting, something that lifts our spirits.
Some dreams are mere fancy, but others
are meant to last a lifetime because God
embedded them in our hearts. It's when we
lose sight of those dreams that hope dies.

But God offers us access to His almighty
power—the very same greatness that brought
His Son back from the dead. What greater
hope is there?

Make the Most

Since everything will be destroyed in this way, what kind of people ought you to be? You ought to live holy and godly lives.

2 PETER 3:11 NIV

Knowing that the world will not last forever, how should we act? We have no devil-may-care option, in which we act as if eternity does not matter, because God calls us to live wholly for Him. The world's destruction should not make us careless, but vigilant to make the most of our time. In the end, all we do here will not be lost but will pass on into eternity.

True Success

"For I know the plans I have for you,"
*declares the L*ORD*, "plans to prosper*
you. . .plans to give you
hope and a future."
JEREMIAH 29:11 NIV

A s little girls, we dream about the handsome man we'll one day marry, exciting trips we'll take, the mansion we'll call home, and the beautiful, perfect children we'll have. A successful life—isn't that what we hope for?

But God doesn't call us to be successful; He calls us to trust Him. We may never be successful in the world's eyes, but trust in our Father's omnipotence ensures our future and our hope. And that's true success.

You Have Gifts!

Now to each one the manifestation of the Spirit is given for the common good.

1 CORINTHIANS 12:7 NIV

Did you know that you are a gifted person? God gives each of His children spiritual gifts designed to help themselves and others— wisdom, knowledge, faith, healing, to name just a few. As you grow spiritually, you begin to unwrap those presents from God. Over time you may be surprised and blessed at how many He's provided for you.

Feeling unimportant? Remind yourself that you're gifted by God!

I Can't Lose!

*Alive, I'm Christ's messenger; dead,
I'm his bounty. Life versus even
more life! I can't lose.*

PHILIPPIANS 1:21 MSG

The old-timer smiled at his granddaughter as
she rebuked him for driving the farm tractor.
"Don't you know the danger at your age,
Grandpa? You could be killed!"

"I'm not worried, darlin', and you
shouldn't be either. What's the worst that
could happen? I wake up in heaven. This life
versus an even better one. . .for all eternity."

When worry begins to overshadow hope,
remember three little words from Philippians:
I can't lose!

Eternal Blessings

A faithful man will abound with blessings,
but he who hastens to be rich
will not go unpunished.

PROVERBS 28:20 NKJV

Faithfulness to God or success in the world:
Have you had to choose between them?
Seeking the world's goals brings short-term
benefits, but only God provides abundant and
ongoing blessings for those who put serving
Him first in their lives. Though worldly
blessings last for a day, a year, or a few years,
they cannot remain for eternity. When you
consider success, think of the kind that really
lasts.

Easy as ABC

*God has done all this, so that we will look
for him and reach out and find him.
He isn't far from any of us.*

ACTS 17:27 CEV

God is near. But we must reach out for Him.
There's a line that we choose to cross, a
specific action we take. We can't ooze into the
kingdom of God; it's an intentional decision.
It's simple, really—as simple as ABC. A is
Admitting we're sinful and in need of a Savior.
B is Believing that Jesus died for our sins and
rose from the grave. C is Committing our lives
to Him. Life everlasting is then ours.

Living in Him

❦

*The meek will inherit the land
and enjoy peace and prosperity.*

PSALM 37:11 NIV

———————————

You might call this God's definition of
success: a profitable land that provides for His
people and His peace that provides a blessed
life. Notice that money and other possessions
aren't mentioned. But the peace of living in
Him flows freely to those who abide in Him.
Would this be success to you? If not, what
does it tell you about your spiritual life?

Best Seller

The mystery is that Christ lives in you,
and he is your hope of sharing in God's glory.
COLOSSIANS 1:27 CEV

Everybody loves a good mystery—as long as
the plot twists a bit and the good guy wins in
the end. The Christian life is a mystery. It's
baffling that God could love us so deeply that
He sent His only Son to suffer and die for us.
And now the risen Christ lives in our hearts,
bridging the gap between us and God forever.
What an incredible page-turner!

Ask Jesus

Because he himself suffered when he was tempted, he is able to help those who are being tempted.

<small>HEBREWS 2:18 NIV</small>

Why can Jesus help us when temptation strikes? Because He's walked a mile in our shoes. He knows how strongly sin attracts us. But because He never fell prey to it, He can effectively show us how to resist even the strongest enticement. The biggest mistakes we make are not calling on Him and not persistently seeking His powerful aid when Satan repeatedly lures us into sin. Need help? Just ask Jesus.

Survivor

❧❧❧

The terrible storm raged for many
days. . .until at last all hope was gone.
ACTS 27:20 NLT

Following a lovely renewal of our wedding
vows on our tenth anniversary, my husband
and I boarded a Caribbean cruise ship.
Tragically, Hurricane Gilbert obliterated our
destination, Cancun, before hurling our ship
back and forth on twelve-foot waves for four
interminable days. I felt hopeless, sick as a
pup, and at the mercy of the storm. Life's like
that, isn't it? Unexpected storms blow up, blot
out the light, and toss us about. But we are
survivors!

God's Protection

*The Lord knows how to deliver the godly
out of temptations and to reserve the unjust
under punishment for the day of judgment.*

2 PETER 2:9 NKJV

Feeling surrounded by temptations? God
hasn't forgotten you. He knows how to
protect His children from harm and offers
His wisdom to His children. Maybe you need
to avoid places that could lead you into sin—
that may mean taking action like finding a
new job or new friends. When God is trying
to protect you, don't resist. Sin is never better
than knowing Him.

Prune Juice, Anyone?

*Therefore, with minds that are alert and
fully sober, set your hope on the grace to be
brought to you when Jesus Christ is revealed.*

1 PETER 1:13 NIV

Diets are the devil. They exclude chocolate
éclairs and hinge on effective use of that
dreaded *s* word: self-control. In the fruit bowl
of the Spirit, self-control is the prune. It's hard
to swallow but nonetheless essential to our
faith—especially where hope is concerned. If
self-control isn't exercised, we can find our
spirits soaring up and down faster than the
numbers on our bathroom scales. Like prunes,
daily use of self-control regulates us and
prepares us for action.

Give Thanks

❧⟡❧

Give thanks to the God of gods.
His love endures forever.
PSALM 136:2 NIV

Having trouble being thankful? Read Psalm
136. You'll be reminded of the wonders of
God's power and His enduring love. The God
who protected Israel watches over you, too.
Even when there may be little in your life to
rejoice about, you can always delight in Him.
Give thanks to God. He has not forgotten
you—His love endures forever.

True Colors

May integrity and honesty protect me,
for I put my hope in you.
PSALM 25:21 NLT

_____

At first the raven appeared solid black, but when she perched in a shaft of sunlight, her feathers shimmered in iridescent emerald, turquoise, and teal: her true colors.

We sometimes hide little acts of dishonesty—taking the bank's pen, pocketing that extra dollar from the clerk's mistake, fudging tax figures. But our integrity is on display at all times to the One who gave His life for us. When our true colors are exposed in the Son-light, we want to shimmer, too.

DAY 196

God Saves

I will give you thanks, for you answered me; you have become my salvation.

PSALM 118:21 NIV

A new believer didn't write this verse. The psalmist thanks God not just for loving Him enough to tear Him from the claws of original sin; instead, this mature man of faith recognizes that God saves him every day, whenever he is in trouble. God does this in your life, too. What salvation has He worked in your life recently? What thanks do you need to offer Him now?

Creating a Chalice

"We live by faith, not by sight."
2 CORINTHIANS 5:7 NIV

Okay, so you popped a tire and the boss exploded because you were late for work again. Your dog upchucked in front of the dinner guests. Your daughter failed the big test. Your elderly mother fell and broke her hip. Bill collectors recite your number by heart. That's the outside. On the inside, God is sanding your sharp edges—impatience, frustration, worry—into a smooth chalice filled with His grace.

Eternal Appreciation

LORD my God,
I will praise you forever.
PSALM 30:12 NIV

Even in eternity, you will be thanking God. The appreciation of God's mercy by His people never stops. Without His grace, we would be forever separated from Him, lost in the cares of sin and a hellish existence. The bliss of a heavenly eternity could not be our inheritance.

Could you thank Jesus too much now? Or could you ever find enough words to show Him your love? Maybe it's time to get started on your eternal appreciation of your Lord.

Integrity

✦✦✦✦✦

*"Is not your fear of God your confidence, and
the integrity of your ways your hope?"*

JOB 4:6 NASB

———————

"Live your faith." These three little words are
the goal of every Christian. Not "Don't smoke,
cuss, or chew or hang around with those
who do," or even "Be good so you'll get into
heaven." Integrity begets behavior, not the
other way around. We want to please our Lord
by righteous behavior so we can fulfill the
challenge of St. Francis of Assisi: "Preach the
gospel at all times. Use words if necessary."

Look Ahead to Heaven

*For our light and momentary troubles are
achieving for us an eternal glory
that far outweighs them all.*

2 CORINTHIANS 4:17 NIV

———————————

What trouble could you face on earth that
will not seem small in heaven? No pain from
this life will impede you there. Blessing
for faithful service to God will replace each
heartache that discourages you today. When
trials and troubles beset you, look ahead to
heaven. Jesus promises you an eternal reward
if you keep your eyes on Him.

Meet Me There

Christ gives me the strength to face anything.
PHILIPPIANS 4:13 CEV

Most women dread going out alone—to
restaurants, shopping, social events—even
church. Sometimes we are the loneliest when
we're in a crowd. It's intimidating to face a
roomful of strangers. But it's well worth it
to bite the bullet and just go to that church
brunch or spiritual retreat or Bible Study. I
would have missed some awesome blessings if
I hadn't gone (alone) to many spiritual events.
I found I did know somebody after all. Jesus
met me there.

Joy Is Straight Ahead

The genuineness of your faith, being much more precious than gold that perishes, though it is tested by fire, may be found to praise, honor, and glory at the revelation of Jesus Christ.

1 PETER 1:7 NKJV

Trials have a purpose in our lives. As a smith heats up gold to purify it, God heats up our lives to make spiritual impurities rise to the surface. If we cooperate with Him, sin is skimmed off our lives, purifying our faith. Cleansed lives bring glory to God and joy to us. If a trial lies before you today, envision the joy ahead.

Fly Me Away

❧❧❧

But those who hope in the LORD will renew their strength. They will soar on wings like eagles; they will run and not grow weary, they will walk and not be faint.

<small>ISAIAH 40:31 NIV</small>

On those weary days when our chins drag the ground, when our feet are stuck fast in the quagmire of everyday responsibility, this verse becomes our hope and our prayer: Mount me up with wings like eagles, Father, fly me away! Let my spirit soar above the clouds on the winds of Your strength. Make me strong as a marathon runner, continuing mile after mile after mile. Be my tailwind, Lord. Amen.

Greater Ways

*For since, in the wisdom of God, the world
through wisdom did not know God,
it pleased God through the foolishness of the
message preached to save those who believe.*

1 Corinthians 1:21 nkjv

To this world, God's wisdom doesn't look
very wise. Anyone who denies Jesus is
blind to the depth of insight God showed
in sending His Son to die for us and then
raising Him from the dead. But those
who accept His sacrifice understand that
God's ways are greater than ours and His
astuteness far outweighs our own. As His
wisdom fills our once-foolish lives, we gain a
new perspective on His perception.

Reboot

*Be strong in the Lord
and in his mighty power.*

EPHESIANS 6:10 NLT

The toilet overflows, check bounces, temper flies, scale shows a three pound gain, kids stampede, husband forgets again. . . .

Ever have one of those days? How marvelous that when we're at our weakest point, our Lord is at His strongest, and He gladly shares that strength with us. He won't necessarily fix the plumbing, but He will reboot our attitudes.

Wise Humility

❧━━━━❧

Woe unto them that are wise in their own eyes, and prudent in their own sight!

ISAIAH 5:21 KJV

Wisdom without humility isn't wisdom at all. When we feel astute under our own power, we are actually in big trouble and are heading into foolishness! The truly wise person recognizes that all wisdom comes from God, not frail humans. As we tap into His mind and connect with His astuteness, we are wise indeed. There is no one wiser than He.

Fearfully Made

You knit me together in my mother's womb.
I praise you because I am fearfully
and wonderfully made.

PSALM 139:13–14 NIV

Crow's feet, frizzy hair, saddle bags, big feet—most women dislike something about their bodies. We feel much more fearfully than wonderfully made. But God loves us just as we are. He wants us to look past the wrinkles and see laugh footprints; to use those knobby knees for praying and age-spotted hands for serving. And in the process, praise Him for limbs that move, eyes that see, and ears that hear His Word.

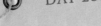

Wise Words

She speaks with wisdom, and faithful instruction is on her tongue.

PROVERBS 31:26 NIV

The virtuous woman's mouth speaks kindly wisdom. Hers is no sharp tongue that destroys relationships. As we seek to do God's will, truthful yet caring speech must be ours. Wise words heal hurting hearts. If we have trouble knowing what words bring God's healing, we need only to ask Him to let His Spirit bring wisdom and kindness to our mouths and tongues. When we speak as His Spirit directs, we are wise indeed.

Send Me a Sign

Let your unfailing love surround us,
Lord, for our hope is in you alone.
PSALM 33:22 NLT

With deadlines and schedules swirling in my
head while driving down the interstate, I did
a double take at the car passing me. A white-
painted message across the back passenger
window grabbed my attention: I am loved.
Wow. So am I. It only took a moment to thank
Papa God for His unfailing love, but a smile
lit my face all day. A simple but profound
reminder is all we need from time to time.

Share His Love

I pray that your partnership with us in the faith may be effective in deepening your understanding of every good thing we share for the sake of Christ.

PHILEMON 1:6 NIV

Many of us have a hard time sharing our faith. So when we hear Paul's encouragement to Philemon, our hearts lift, knowing we aren't the only ones who struggle. Isn't the challenge of witnessing to others worth it once we've read this promise? The salvation of others and our own appreciation of our Lord: Could we have better reasons to share His love?

No Greater Comfort

"O death, where is your victory?
O death, where is your sting?"

1 CORINTHIANS 15:55 NLT

———————————

There's no denying that the loss of a loved one stings. Our hearts burn, sear, and ache with pain. But Christ's victory over death after His crucifixion enables His followers to experience that same victory. We, too, will stand as conquerors of the grave, arm in arm with believers who have gone before us. What greater hope? What greater comfort?

Shine On

❧✦❧

*"You are the light of the world.
A town built on a hill cannot be hidden."*
MATTHEW 5:14 NIV

God means you to be a light set where the
world can see it clearly—not a hidden flame
behind closed doors, with curtains drawn.
Being a light isn't always easy—people see
everything you do, and they don't always
like it. Don't let the critics stop you. Your
works were ordained to glorify God, not make
people comfortable. Knowing that, are you
ready to shine today?

Laugh a Rainbow

"When I see the rainbow in the clouds,
I will remember the eternal covenant between
God and every living creature on earth."
GENESIS 9:16 NLT

Ever feel like a cloud is hanging over your
head? Sometimes the cloud darkens to the
color of bruises, and we're deluged with cold
rain that seems to have no end. When you're
in the midst of one of life's thunderstorms,
tape this saying to your mirror: Cry a river,
laugh a rainbow. The rainbow, the symbol
of hope that God gave Noah after the flood,
reminds us even today that every storm will
eventually pass.

Kind Words

*Let your speech always be with grace,
seasoned with salt, that you may know
how you ought to answer each one.*

COLOSSIANS 4:6 NKJV

Your words are a vital part of your witness.
Speak to an unbeliever ungraciously, and
chances are good that she will never forget it.
But study and grow in the Word; then speak
wisely and generously to others, and God can
use your words to win them to His kingdom.
People respond well to kindness and flavorful
speech. What are your words saying today?

Asking Why?

God will never forget the needy;
the hope of the afflicted will never perish.
PSALM 9:18 NIV

Why me? Why is God allowing this to
happen? Why doesn't He intervene?

When we're in the midst of a difficult time,
it's easy to forget that God is not the afflicter,
but is the helper and healer of the afflicted. He
is not cracking the whip but feels every stripe
inflicted on our backs by a sin-filled world—
just like those of His only Son, Jesus.

Turn from Wrong

*There is therefore now no condemnation
to those who are in Christ Jesus,
who do not walk according to the flesh,
but according to the Spirit.*

ROMANS 8:1 NKJV

No condemnation! What a wonderful thought
for sinners! Forgiven, we know the comfort
of having heaven as our ultimate destination.
But have we also read the second part of the
verse? This is no blanket agreement that
okays sin. The joy of our freedom must lead
us to turn from all wrong. Our Lord gives the
strength to grow in Him.

Tune In

And hope does not put us to shame,
because God's love has been poured out
into our hearts through the Holy Spirit,
who has been given to us.

ROMANS 5:5 NIV

Is your spiritual antenna tuned in to the Holy
Spirit? The Holy Spirit is the communicator
of the trinity: our helper, comforter, and
instructor. Through Him, God pours love and
hope into us. Like radio waves broadcasting
invisibly through the atmosphere, the Holy
Spirit communicates to believers. We must,
however, make the effort to tune in our
receivers to His frequency, and then choose
to obey His guidance—even when it's
inconvenient.

Inheritors of Earth

*"Blessed are the meek,
for they will inherit the earth."*
MATTHEW 5:5 NIV

In the workplace, meekness isn't often seen as a positive thing. "Looking out for number one" is the theory of many who tout assertiveness as the way to get the most out of life.

But God doesn't say that. Ultimately those who follow Him faithfully and show their belief to the world will not be the "nice guys" who "finish last," but the inheritors of this earth. What plot of earth might God have mapped out for you?

Saints Preserve Us

*I will always praise you
in the presence of your faithful people.*
PSALM 52:9 NIV

We sing, "Lord, I want to be in that number, when the saints go marching in!" But who exactly are saints? Exceptionally good people like Saint Nicholas or Mother Teresa? The Bible calls all true believers saints. Some think if their derriere simply graces a pew, they're in. But sitting in church no more makes you a Christian than standing in your closet makes you a vacuum cleaner. Only dedicated Christ-lovers will march into heaven. Are you in that number?

DAY 220

Everything for God

❧✦❧

*Whatever you do, work at it with all your
heart, as working for the Lord.*
COLOSSIANS 3:23 NIV

Did you know you are not really working for
your boss? Yes, you report to the one whom
your company hired in that position, but
ultimately you do everything for God, not
a man or woman. So even if your boss isn't
great to work for, remind yourself that you
are accountable to Jesus. No matter who has
the position above yours, your Lord is always
in charge of your future.

If You Build It, He Will Come

Do not snatch your word of truth from me,
for your regulations are my only hope.
PSALM 119:43 NLT

Bibles wear and tear. Papers get discarded.
Hard drives crash. But memorizing scripture
assures us that God's Word will never be lost.
His truth will always be at our disposal, any
moment of the day or night when we need a
word of encouragement, of guidance, of hope.
Like a phone call from heaven, our Father
communicates to us via scripture implanted in
our hearts. But it is up to us to build the signal
tower.

Serious Business

Make it your ambition to lead a quiet life:
You should mind your own business
and work with your hands.

1 THESSALONIANS 4:11 NIV

Whether we work at a computer or on a
factory production line, those of us who work
with our hands shouldn't feel unimportant.
Manual labor is serious business in God's
sight. Christians who quietly, faithfully
go about their business day by day make
an important contribution, bearing God's
message to a wide range of people. What a
testimony our lives become when we live out
this verse.

Blameless

*[Jesus] has brought you into his own
presence, and you are holy and blameless as
you stand before him without a single fault.*

COLOSSIANS 1:22 NLT

Holiness. Wouldn't we all like to attain it? But
it's impossible. Even if we shave our heads,
eat only birdseed, forsake makeup, and wear
nothing but mumus, we still wouldn't be holy.
We'd just be ugly. The only way we can achieve
holiness is through Jesus, who by His death on
our behalf ushers us into the presence of God,
blameless, beautiful, and whole. And we can
leave our mumus at home.

More Than Temporary

Do not be afraid when one becomes rich,
when the glory of his house is increased;
for when he dies he shall carry nothing
away; his glory shall not descend after him.

PSALM 49:16–17 NKJV

This is the Bible's way of saying, "You can't
take it with you." When life ends, the only
treasures that remain are the works we
have done for Jesus. Money and fame cling
to earth, soon to be forgotten. So when
unbelievers seem to get all the goodies,
we just remember that the treasures we
send ahead to heaven are greater than any
temporary gain.

Whole and Healed

Pray for each other so that you can live together whole and healed. The prayer of a person living right with God is something powerful to be reckoned with.

JAMES 5:16 MSG

Do you have soul siblings? Brothers and sisters in Christ? Caring people who pray for you and with you about, well, everything? Like a life preserver in a turbulent sea, prayer partners are buoyancy for the soul and security through any storm. Heart-bonds, once established, create a trusting environment where we can bare our souls before the Lord in mutual prayer to become whole and healed. Prayer partners are warm hugs from God.

Belong to Jesus

"If you belonged to the world, it would love you as its own. As it is, you do not belong to the world, but I have chosen you out of the world. That is why the world hates you."

JOHN 15:19 NIV

Don't expect the world to love you for loving Jesus. Because He doesn't accept its evil, and neither do you, the world is at enmity with both of you. That's not such a bad thing. Who would you rather belong to: Jesus, who holds eternity's joys in His hands, or the world, which offers so much sin and pain?

Slathered in SPF

You are my refuge and my shield;
I have put my hope in your word.

PSALM 119:114 NIV

These days, the word shield evokes images
of glistening sunbathers dotting beaches
and carefree children slathered in sunscreen.
Like the psalmist's metal shield, sunscreen
deflects dangerous rays, preventing them from
penetrating vulnerable skin—higher SPF for
more protection. When we are immersed in
God's Word, we erect a shield that deflects
Satan's attempts to penetrate our weak flesh.
Internalizing more of God's Word creates a
higher SPF: Scripture Protection Factor. Are
you well-coated?

A Prayerful Solution

I want the men everywhere to pray,
lifting up holy hands without
anger or disputing.

1 TIMOTHY 2:8 NIV

Anger becomes a real trap, even for
Christians. When we try to settle differences
angrily, we land in big trouble, affecting and
even destroying a whole congregation. One
solution to anger is prayer. It's hard to stay
angry with someone you pray for, even if that
person continues to irritate you. As God's
Spirit works in your heart, you give the other
person a second, a third, or even a hundred
and third chance. In Jesus, unrighteous anger
cannot linger.

The Foundation and Finale

*I hope to see you soon, and then we will
talk face to face. Peace be with you.*

3 JOHN 1:14–15 NLT

My prayer is that the message you receive
from this book is that Christ is the ultimate
source of hope. We can live without many
things, but we cannot live without hope. It's
the air we breathe, the water that invigorates
every molecule of our being, the motivation
that drives us. Hope enriches and empowers
us, connecting us with our Papa God. Hope
is the essence of our faith. It's the foundation
and the finale.

Letting Go of Anger

❧

Now the works of the flesh are evident,
which are: adultery. . .idolatry,
sorcery, hatred, contentions,
jealousies, outbursts of wrath.

GALATIANS 5:19–20 NKJV

It's not something we like to hear, but according to God, anger is right up there with sins such as adultery and idolatry.

Most of us feel wrathful occasionally. But if such feelings take hold of our lives and bitterness results, we fall into sin. When anger touches our reactions, let's use it as a warning sign of an issue that requires our attention. Through wise action and prayer, it need not control us.

Shouts of Joy

❧❦❧

*He will yet fill your mouth with laughter
and your lips with shouts of joy.*

JOB 8:21 NIV

Do you remember the last time you laughed
till you cried? For many of us, it's been far too
long. Stress tends to steal our joy, leaving us
humorless and oh-so-serious. But lightness
and fun haven't disappeared forever. They
may be buried beneath the snow of a long,
wintery life season, but spring is coming, girls.
Laughter will bloom again, and our hearts
will soar as our lips shout with joy. Grasp that
hope!

Today!

*"Therefore do not worry about tomorrow,
for tomorrow will worry about itself.
Each day has enough trouble of its own."*

MATTHEW 6:34 NIV

You can look ahead and obsess about fears for the future or take life one day at a time and enjoy it. But you only live in today, not in the weeks, months, and years that may lie ahead. You can only change life in the moment you're in now. Since worry never improves the future and only hurts today, you'll benefit most from trusting in God and enjoying the spot where He's planted you for now.

I'm No Eeyore

❧❧❧❧

Then [Job's] wife said to him, "Do you still hold fast your integrity? Curse God and die!"
JOB 2:9 NASB

Job's wife was the unwilling recipient of Satan's attacks because of her husband's righteous life. When the going got tough, our girl lost faith and hope disintegrated. We, too, sometimes lose sight of all God has done for us and focus only on what He hasn't done. Our optimistic attitudes are consumed by negativity. Job's response is the key to escaping the shackles of Eeyore-ism: "I know that my Redeemer lives" (Job 19:25 NASB).

Sharing with Jesus

*Casting all your care upon him;
for he careth for you.*
1 PETER 5:7 KJV

You don't have a care in the world that you
cannot share—with Jesus, that is. There isn't
one thing He doesn't want to hear about
from you. Before you ask a friend to pray for
you (and you should do that), be certain you
share your care with your best Friend, Jesus.
Your human friend may try to help you and
may do a lot for you, but no one helps like
Jesus. There's no worry He can't alleviate or
remove.

Confounded Corsets

*Cultivate inner beauty, the gentle,
gracious kind that God delights in.*

1 PETER 3:4 MSG

In our quest for beauty, we buy into all sorts
of crazy things: mud facials, cosmetic surgery,
body piercings, obsessive dieting, squeezing
size 10 feet into size 8 shoes. The image of
Scarlett O'Hara's binding corset makes us
shudder. (Reminds me of a pair of jeans I
wrestled with just last week.) Yet God's idea
of beauty is on the inside—where spandex
cannot touch. Let's resolve to devote more
time pursuing inner beauty that will never
require Botox.

DAY 236

Powerful Prayer

*"The LORD bless you and keep you;
the LORD make his face shine on
you and be gracious to you."*
NUMBERS 6:24–25 NIV

Want to pray for someone? This is a good way
to do it. It's the blessing God gave to Aaron
and his sons to pronounce on Israel. What
Christian wouldn't appreciate these words,
committing her to God's care and wanting
her to draw closer to Him? Who would turn
down the good things God has to offer? Can
you bless your friends and family with these
thoughts today?

Good Enough

❦

Leah's eyes were weak, but Rachel
was beautiful of form and face.
GENESIS 29:17 NASB

Have you ever felt like a booby prize? No
doubt Leah did. Hunky Jacob labored seven
years to marry Leah's gorgeous sister, Rachel.
Then their squirrelly father switched his
daughters at the altar. Jacob freaked. Leah
tanked. We, too, sometimes feel that we're not
good enough—that we don't measure up. But
Leah gave birth to six of the twelve tribes of
Israel, the cornerstone of Judeo-Christendom.
God has a mighty plan for all of us Leahs.

Living for Christ

If you live according to the flesh, you will die; but if by the Spirit you put to death the misdeeds of the body, you will live.

ROMANS 8:13 NIV

Living for Christ through His Spirit offers real life, overflowing and abundant. Blessings spill over in obedient lives. But the world, at war with God, doesn't understand. Unbelievers never feel the touch of the Spirit in their hearts and lives, and Jesus' gentle love is foreign to them. Put to death worldly misdeeds, and instead of the emptiness of the world, you'll receive blessings indeed.

A Little Goes a Long Way

❧

*"The LORD our God has allowed a few
of us to survive as a remnant."*
EZRA 9:8 NLT

Remnants. Useless by most standards, but
God is in the business of using tiny slivers of
what's left to do mighty things. Nehemiah
rebuilt the fallen walls of Jerusalem with
a remnant of Israel; Noah's three sons
repopulated the earth after the flood; four
slave boys—Daniel, Shadrach, Meshach,
and Abednego—kept faith alive for an entire
nation. When it feels as if bits and pieces are
all that has survived of your hope, remember
how much God can accomplish with
remnants!

An Obedient Life

*How blessed are those whose way is
blameless, who walk in the law of the LORD.*
PSALM 119:1 NASB

Want to be blessed? Then don't live a sin-
filled life. God can't pour out blessings
on anyone who consistently ignores His
commands. Blessings belong to those who
hear God's Word and take it to heart, living
it out in love. Want to be blessed? Obey the
Master. You'll live blamelessly and joyfully.

The SAM Creed

*If we are thrown into the blazing furnace,
the God we serve is able to save us. . . .
But even if he doesn't. . .we will
never serve your gods.*
DANIEL 3:17–18 NLT

Shadrach, Meshach, and Abednego were Israeli
boys who were captured and transported as
slaves to Babylon. Ordered by their new king
to worship his god or die horribly in a fiery
furnace, the boys evoked the SAM Creed, an
acronym for their names: My God is able to
deliver me, but even if He chooses not to, I
will still follow Him. Through tough times,
let's resolve to live by The SAM Creed.

See Ya, Self

> *"Blessed are the poor in spirit,*
> *for theirs is the kingdom of heaven."*
> MATTHEW 5:3 NASB

We don't often think of ourselves as "poor in spirit," but this passage refers to those who are not full of themselves; those who are filled instead with God's spirit. "Poor" in this context means selfless rather than selfish; those with an attitude of dependence on God. How do we become poor in spirit and revel in the hope and promise of heaven? By emptying ourselves of self and the pride of self-sufficiency, and refilling ourselves with Jesus.

The Gift of Children

*Children are a heritage from the LORD,
offspring a reward from him.*
PSALM 127:3 NIV

Today many people see children more as a
punishment than a reward. But when you
hear of parents who wish they had never had
children, you know they're missing out. God
creates families to love each other and share
His joys. Parents who honestly live out their
faith before their children can also guide them
into a good family life. Are your children a
blessing? He's given them as a reward, not as a
punishment. Do you treat them that way?

Cat-a-tude Versus Dog-a-tude

❧⨾❧

May those who hope in you not be disgraced because of me; God of Israel.
PSALM 69:6 NIV

Are you a hisser or a wagger?

Perhaps you have a feline attitude: It's all about me. I like you for what you can do for me. You'll have my attention only when it's convenient for me. Me, me, me.

Or maybe you have a dog mentality: It's all about you. I love you unconditionally just because you're you. How can I make you happy?

God is glorified by selflessness, not selfishness. Let's strive to make our Master proud.

Wise Correction

A rod and a reprimand impart wisdom,
but a child left undisciplined
disgraces its mother.

PROVERBS 29:15 NIV

In today's world, fears of child abuse have
caused us to ignore this verse. Have we
therefore missed the power of correction,
which gives our children wisdom? As God
restrains us from wrongdoing, we need to
stop our children, too. We need not touch
a child physically to modify behavior. Will
we discipline harmful actions now or lose
the chance to be proud of our self-controlled
children who love the Lord?

Comforting the Comfortless

He brings us alongside someone else who is going through hard times so that we can be there for that person just as God was there for us.

2 CORINTHIANS 1:4 MSG

Heartbroken and hollow after my sixth miscarriage, I struggled to find meaning in my loss. My heavenly Father's arms comforted me when I burst into tears at song lyrics or at the sight of a mother cuddling her infant in WalMart. I finally relinquished my babies to Jesus' loving embrace, confident that I'd see them again one day. I was then able to share His comfort and hope with other women suffering miscarriages.

Reaching Out

❧

*For just as we share abundantly in the
sufferings of Christ, so also our
comfort abounds through Christ.*

2 Corinthians 1:5 niv

Paul knew the pain of persecution, but he also
knew the deep comfort God offered. When
people gave the apostle trouble, God drew
His servant close to His heart. When trials
come your way, God will do the same for you.
If life is always going smoothly, comfort is
meaningless, but when you're in the midst of
trouble, He comes alongside with tender love
that overflows your trials and reaches out to
others.

Loose Lips

*We all make many mistakes. For if we
could control our tongues, we would
be perfect and could also control
ourselves in every other way.*

JAMES 3:2 NLT

Many of us don't let thoughts marinate long
before we spew them out of our mouths.
We want to honor God with our speech but
seem to spend more time dousing forest fires
resulting from sparks kindled by our wagging
tongues (James 3:5). Don't despair! There's
hope for loose lips! The Creator of self-
control is happy to loan us a muzzle (Psalm
39:1) if we sincerely want to change.

Renewal of Faith

*"As one whom his mother comforts,
so I will comfort you."*

ISAIAH 66:13 NKJV

Like a tender mother, God comforts His
people. When life challenges us, we have
a place to renew our faith. Instead of
questioning God's compassion because we
face a trial, we can draw ever nearer to Him,
seeking to do His will. Surrounded by His
tender arms, we gain strength to go out and
face the world again.

DAY 250

The Eyes Have It

All of you together are Christ's body,
and each of you is a part of it.
1 CORINTHIANS 12:27 NLT

Just as our bodies are compiled of many parts,
each essential for functioning as a whole, the
body of Christ is made up of hands, feet, ears,
hearts, and minds. We women understand
this concept but tend to compare ourselves
to others. If we're hands, we wish we were
feet. If we're noses, we'd rather be eyes.
Sometimes we feel like bunions. But God
views us as equally important, none better
than another. Even us toenails!

Giver of Comfort

❦

*You ought to forgive and comfort him,
so that he will not be overwhelmed
by excessive sorrow.*

2 CORINTHIANS 2:7 NIV

Do you know someone who is sorry for her
sin? Then don't keep reminding her of it. If
she has sought forgiveness and put it behind
her, it is dead. Instead of criticizing, remind
her of the power of God that works in her
life. Encourage her when temptation calls
her name. Then she will not be overcome by
sorrow and fall into sin again. Give comfort,
and you will be a blessing.

Holding Hands

❧⟡❧

When I am afraid,
I will put my trust in You.

PSALM 56:3 NASB

While I cowered in a bathroom stall before
my first speaking event, my queasy stomach
rolled and sweat beaded on my forehead.
I prayed for a way to escape. Into my head
popped a childhood memory verse: "When
I am afraid, I will put my trust in You."
My pounding heart calmed. I repeated the
scripture aloud and felt my nausea subside
and panic diminish. Peace flooded my soul.
When we're afraid, Papa God is right beside
us holding our hand.

God's Provision

*Now godliness with
contentment is great gain.*

1 TIMOTHY 6:6 NKJV

Paul warned Timothy against false teachers
who wanted to use the church for financial
gain. If these people were looking for security,
they were on the wrong track. Money, which
comes and goes, never brings real protection.
Our security lies in God's provision. Whether
or not we have a large bank account, we can
feel content in Jesus. The One who brought
us into this world will never forget we require
food, clothing, and all the rest. When we truly
trust in Jesus, contentment is sure to follow.

Down with Flab

*Workouts in the gymnasium are useful,
but a disciplined life in God is far more so,
making you fit both today and forever.*

1 TIMOTHY 4:7–8 MSG

Do you have Dumbo flaps? You know, those
fleshy wings that hang on the underside of your
arms when you raise them. A stiff wind could
create liftoff. They say regular workouts will
tighten those puppies up. . .and significantly
reduce wind shear. Just as we exercise muscles
to make them strong, we keep our faith in
shape by exercising it. Discipline is the way to
conquer flab—physically and spiritually!

Contentment in Trouble

The fear of the LORD leads to life: then one rests content, untouched by trouble.
PROVERBS 19:23 NIV

God doesn't promise we will never suffer trouble, but He does promise something even more important. In the middle of trouble, we will experience real life contentment in the middle of confusion, doubt, or turmoil. Which would you prefer, trouble and life in Jesus, or trouble on its own? You can't avoid trouble here on earth. But share life with Him, and contentment will follow.

Bigger than Fear

Having hope will give you courage. You will be protected and will rest in safety.

JOB 11:18 NLT

Tossing, turning, sleepless nights: What woman doesn't know these intimately? Our thoughts race with the "what if's" and fear steals our peace. How precious is God's promise that He will rescue us from nagging, faceless fear and give us courage to just say no to anxious thoughts that threaten to terrorize us at our most vulnerable moments. He is our hope and protector. He is bigger than fear. Anxiety flees in His presence. Rest with Him tonight.

Eternal Perspective

*"Where, O death, is your victory?
Where, O death, is your sting?"*

1 CORINTHIANS 15:55 NIV

Nothing in this world ameliorates the pain
of death. Losing one we love reaches deep
into our souls. But with His sacrifice, Jesus
permanently overcame the sting of mortality.
Those who trust in Him do not live for a few
short years, but for eternity. When sin takes
their lives, they simply move into heaven.

When we lose loved ones, our hearts feel
pain. But if they gave their lives to Jesus, He
is still victorious. In time we will meet them
again in paradise.

Smiling in the Darkness

The hopes of the godless evaporate.
JOB 8:13 NLT

Hope isn't just an emotion; it's a perspective, a discipline, a way of life. It's a journey of choice. We must learn to override those messages of discouragement, despair, and fear that assault us in times of trouble and press toward the light. Hope is smiling in the darkness. It's confidence that faith in God's sovereignty amounts to something. . .something life-changing, life-saving, and eternal.

Death Will Die

The last enemy to be destroyed is death.
1 CORINTHIANS 15:26 NIV

If Jesus conquered death, why do we still
suffer with loved ones dying? Because today
we live in the promise of death's destruction,
not its completion. God's Son has ransomed
us through His sacrifice, but death still exists
in our world. One day, that will no longer be
so. Jesus promises to destroy death entirely—
death shall die, and heaven will be ours.

Let Me Be

"Martha...you are worried and upset about many things, but few things are needed— or indeed only one. Mary has chosen what is better."

LUKE 10:41–42 NIV

Martha zipped around cleaning, cooking, and organizing. Meanwhile, Mary sat at Jesus' feet. Many of us think like Martha. Will food magically appear on the table? Will the house clean itself? We're slaves to endless to-do lists. Our need to *do* overwhelms our desire to *be*. Constipated calendars attest that we are human doings instead of human beings. But Jesus taught that Mary chose best—simply to be. Lord, help this doer learn to be.

Be Faithful

Good and upright is the LORD;
therefore he instructs sinners in his ways.

PSALM 25:8 NIV

Don't know which way to turn or where to
go? God will show you. Just be faithful to
Him, and you will hear His still, small voice
guiding you; otherwise, circumstances and
wise advisers will illuminate the path you need
to walk on.

Still doubting? Ask God for forgiveness
for sins that bar your communion with Him.
Soon, with a clean heart, you'll be headed in
the right direction.

Dwelling Place

*Do you not know that you are a temple
of God and that the Spirit
of God dwells in you?*

1 CORINTHIANS 3:16 NASB

Have you ever been awed by the beauty of
a majestic cathedral with towering ceilings
inlaid with gold and silver, magnificent
paintings, rich carpets, and stained glass
windows? Only the finest for the house of
God Almighty.

Did you know God thinks of you and me
as living cathedrals—dwelling places of His
Spirit? How amazing to be considered worthy
of such an honor! How immeasurable His
love to choose us as His dwelling place!

Moving Mountains

"Whoever says to this mountain,
'Be removed and be cast into the sea,'
and does not doubt. . .but believes. . .
will have whatever he says."

MARK 11:23 NKJV

Don't you wish you had faith like this?

Christians often try to gear up to it, willing it with all their hearts. But that's not what God had in mind. Manipulating Him cannot work.

Only when we fully trust in Him will He move our mountain—even if it's in an unexpected direction.

Brick by Brick

*So then faith cometh by hearing,
and hearing by the word of God.*

ROMANS 10:17 KJV

Words are powerful. They cut. They heal.
They confirm. God uses His Word to help us,
to mold us, to make us more like Him. Our
faith is built from the bricks of God's Word.
Brick by brick, we erect, strengthen, and
fortify that faith. But only if we truly listen
and hear the Word of God.

Be Prepared

He has also set eternity in the human heart;
yet no one can fathom what God has
done from beginning to end.

ECCLESIASTES 3:11 NIV

Though each of us has a bit of eternity in our
hearts, and we cannot rest unless we know
the Savior, we also cannot fathom the works
of God. That can either make us dissatisfied
and doubtful or relaxed, trusting children who
know their Father is in control and will care
for them from beginning to end. Have you
trusted Him who is the Alpha and Omega?
Are you prepared for eternity with Him?

Enduring with Grace

Endurance builds character, which gives us a hope that will never disappoint us.

ROMANS 5:4–5 CEV

Heroes come in all packages. My eighteen-year-old niece, Andie, has cerebral palsy and is legally blind. It takes her four times longer than the average person to do just about anything. But she does it anyway: playing drums, walking in leg braces, attending college. Some days, the frustration of being different overwhelms her. But through endurance, she has developed inspiring character traits—rock solid faith, contagious hope, and a stellar sense of humor. When I grow up, I want to be like Andie.

The Christian Life

*Clearly no one who relies on the law
is justified before God, because
"the righteous will live by faith."*

GALATIANS 3:11 NIV

Though some might claim it, crossing all
your t's and dotting your i's spiritually does
not make you a great Christian. Rules and
regulations aren't what the Christian life is
about—faith is. Obeying God and following
Him as the Spirit leads challenges you to trust
Him every moment of your life. With that
kind of belief, you'll share His world-changing
message.

Small but Mighty

He has…exalted the humble.
LUKE 1:52 NLT

_____

God delights in making small things great.
He's in the business of taking scrap-heap
people and turning them into treasures:
Noah (the laughing stock of his city), Moses
(stuttering shepherd turned national leader),
David (smallest among the big and powerful),
Sarah (old and childless), Mary (poor
teenager), Rahab (harlot turned faith-filled
ancestor of Jesus). So you and I can rejoice
with hope! Let us glory in our smallness!

Our Hearts

Are you willing to recognize, you foolish fellow, that faith without works is useless?

JAMES 2:20 NASB

Faith isn't faith if actions don't follow belief. No matter what a person says, unless love, compassion, and kindness accompany her words, it would be foolish to consider her Christian testimony believable.

Though works don't save us, they show what's in our hearts. What are we proving by our works today?

DAY 270

I've Got a Name

I have redeemed you; I have called you by your name; you are Mine.
ISAIAH 43:1 NKJV

Parents have the indescribable privilege of bestowing a name on their newborn. The identity that little person will be known by for the rest of his or her life. In effect, we give them a part of us. They are an extension of ourselves—our flesh, our blood.

Your heavenly Father has called you by name. He has given you part of Himself: Jesus. You are special to Him. You are His daughter. In this, find security. . .comfort. . .hope.

Shine Brightly

*Each one of you also must love his wife
as he loves himself, and the wife must
respect her husband.*

EPHESIANS 5:33 NIV

Marriage is a reciprocal relationship. For it
to work well, both parties have to give and
receive. If you share house space without the
love and respect that make it a home, yours
quickly becomes an empty existence. But
that's not what God had in mind when He
created marriage to reflect His own love for
His people. He can help your marriage shine
brightly for Him, if only you ask Him and are
open to His will.

Jets and Submarines

*No power in the sky above or in the earth
below. . .will ever be able to separate us
from the love of God that is revealed
in Christ Jesus our Lord.*

ROMANS 8:39 NLT

Have you ever been diving amid the
spectacular array of vivid color and teeming
life in the silent world under the sea? Painted
fish of rainbow hues are backlit by diffused
sunbeams. Multi-textured coral dot the
gleaming white sand. You honestly feel as if
you're in another world. But every world is
God's world. He soars above the clouds with
us and spans the depths of the seas. Nothing
can separate us from His love.

The Price of Forgiveness

And according to the law almost all things are purified with blood, and without shedding of blood there is no remission.

HEBREWS 9:22 NKJV

Many people in our world would like cheap forgiveness. They want someone to say they are okay, but they don't want to pay any price for their wrongdoing. That's not what the scriptures say. Remission of sins comes at a high price—sacrificial blood, the blood of Jesus. Jesus says you are worth this expense, and you are clean in Him. Put away sin and rejoice in His deep love for you.

Pick Me Up, Daddy

We boast in the hope of the glory of God.
ROMANS 5:2 NIV

To rejoice means to live joyfully. . .joy-fully
. . .full of joy. Joy is a decision we make. A
choice not to keep wallowing in the mud of
our lives. And there will be mud—at one time
or another. When spiritual rain mixes with
the dirt of fallen people, mud is the inevitable
result. The Creator of sparkling sunbeams,
soaring eagles, and spectacular fuchsia
sunsets wants to lift us out of the mud. Why
don't we raise our arms to Him today?

Pass It On

"If you forgive others for their transgressions, your heavenly Father will also forgive you."

MATTHEW 6:14 NASB

Forgiveness isn't only something God gives us. He designed it to be passed on to others. Doing that, we learn the value of the pardon the Father offered us. Even when everything in us screams, "No, I can't forgive," He empowers us to do so if we trust in Him. Our loving Father never commands us to actions He cannot also strengthen us to do.

His Heart's Delight

The LORD's delight is in those who fear him, those who put their hope in his unfailing love.

PSALM 147:11 NLT

Do you remember how you felt when you witnessed your baby's first faltering steps? Delight. That's what it was. Just like when you heard her sing "Jesus Loves Me" in her squeaky, off-key voice, or she served you tea in tiny pink teacups. The Bible says the Lord delights in us, His children, the very same way. We warm His heart and bring a smile to His lips when we honor Him with our lives. He delights in us.

Importance of Friendship

Do not forsake your friend or a friend of your family, and do not go to your relative's house when disaster strikes you—better a neighbor nearby than a relative far away.

PROVERBS 27:10 NIV

———————————

Friendship is important to God, or He would not encourage us to hold fast to it. As Christians we've known times when other believers seemed closer than our kin. God has brought us into a new family—His own— where faith becomes more important than blood. Through Him our love expands, and we help each other when trouble strikes. No matter where you go, God's people are near.

Rest Stop

*So let's not allow ourselves to get fatigued
doing good. At the right time we
will harvest a good crop if we
don't give up, or quit.*

GALATIANS 6:9 MSG

As women, we're used to serving others. It's
part of the feminine package. But sometimes
we get burned out. Fatigued. Overburdened.
Girls, God doesn't want us to be washed-out
dishrags, to be so boggled that we try to pay
for groceries with our frequent shopper card.
It's up to us to recognize the symptoms and
rest, regroup, reenergize. This is not indulgent;
it's necessary to do our best in His name. So
give yourself permission to rest. Today.

Our Best Friend

*The righteous choose their friends carefully,
but the way of the wicked leads them astray.*
PROVERBS 12:26 NIV

We need friends. But there are those who
will lead us into trouble and those who will
encourage us and lift us up in our faith,
drawing us ever nearer to God. Before we draw
near to others, do we consider their spiritual
impact on us? If God is our best friend, let
us be cautious not to be led astray. When we
share friendship with Jesus and our earthly
friends, we are truly blessed.

Battle Plan

*I sought the LORD, and He answered me,
and delivered me from all my fears.*

PSALM 34:4 NASB

There is nothing more wasteful than fear.
Fear paralyzes, destroys potential, and
shatters hope. It's like an enemy attacking
from our blind side. But we don't have to
allow fear to defeat us. It's a war that we can
win! First comes earnest prayer, then comes
change. God will deliver us from our fears if
we seek Him and follow His battle plan.

Loving Correction

❧❧❧

For whom the LORD loves He corrects,
just as a father the son in whom he delights.

PROVERBS 3:12 NKJV

Do you feel the pain of God's correction?
Take heart, since it shows He loves you. Just
as a loving father will not let his child walk
in a dangerous place, your heavenly Father is
redirecting you onto another path. Today's
discipline may hurt, but in days to come, your
sorrow will turn to joy as you reap the blessing
that follows obedience. Your Father loves you
deeply.

Trumped

*And the L<small>ORD</small> said to Abraham,
"Why did Sarah laugh, saying, 'Shall I
indeed bear a child, when I am so old?'
Is anything too difficult for the L<small>ORD</small>?"*
G<small>ENESIS</small> 18:13–14 NASB

Sarah, well past menopause and losing the drooping appendage war, was so floored when told of her impending pregnancy that she burst into laughter. How absurd to think those breasts sagging to her navel would nurse a baby! But that's exactly what God had in store. We sometimes forget that God created the systems we consider absolute and impenetrable. He can trump them all with a flick of His pinkie!

He Loves You This Much!

See what great love the Father has lavished on us, that we should be called children of God! And that is what we are!

1 JOHN 3:1 NIV

God does not give His love in dribs and drabs. He lavishes it on us when we come to Him in faith. All along, He was waiting to make us His children, and we were the ones who resisted. But once we face Him as His children, God's love lets loose in our lives. Nothing is too good for His obedient children. Praise God that He loves you that much!

One for All

*All of you are part of the same body.
There is only one Spirit of God, just as
you were given one hope when you
were chosen to be God's people.*

EPHESIANS 4:4 CEV

Remember the motto of the Three
Musketeers? "All for one and one for all."
Christ-followers should have the same sense
of unity, for we are bound together by eternal
hope, the gift of our Savior. Feeling with and
for each other, we'll cry tears of joy from
one eye and tears of sadness from the other.
Loneliness is not an option. Take the first
step. Reach out today—someone else's hand
is reaching, too.

Always Faithful

I will never leave thee, nor forsake thee.
HEBREWS 13:5 KJV

Even when fear or stress challenges you, you
need never deal with it single-handedly if
Jesus rules your life. When your life seems in
shambles around you, He offers strength and
comfort for a hurting heart. God never gives
up on you. His love cannot change. Today,
delight in the One who never deserts you.

DAY 286

They're Just Men

"He may have a great army, but they are merely men. We have the Lord our God to help us and to fight our battles for us!"

2 CHRONICLES 32:8 NLT

When facing attack from an enemy army, Hezekiah uttered these profound words: "They're just men. The God of all creation is standing by to fight for us! No comparison!" And sure enough, against all human reasoning, God sent an angel to defeat the entire enemy army (2 Chronicles 32:21). God still intervenes today to help us fight our battles, whether supernaturally or by natural means. Trust Him. He's got His armor on.

Nothing Is Impossible

"For no word from God will ever fail."
LUKE 1:37 NIV

The angel spoke these words to Mary as he gave her the news that the aged Elizabeth would bear a child. God deals with the impossible in our lives, too. We do not bear a Savior, but how has He helped us understand impossible relationships, juggle a hectic schedule, or help a hurting friend? God offers aid, whatever we face. Nothing is impossible for the One at work in our lives. What impossibilities can He deal with in your life? Have you trusted Him for help?

BFF

I am counting on the L<small>ORD</small>;
yes, I am counting on him.
I have put my hope in his word.

P<small>SALM</small> 130:5 <small>NLT</small>

———————————————

"Best Friends Forever" earn this title of
honor because we've learned we can count
on them. They've proven they'll be there for
us through svelte and bloated, sweet and
grumpy, thoughtful and insensitive. Bailing
us out of countless sinking dinghies, they've
held us as we sobbed, fed our families,
watched our kids, and made us smile. How
much more can we count on our Creator to
be there for us?

God Offers Hope

"For I know the plans I have for you,"
declares the Lord, "plans to prosper you
and not to harm you, plans to give
you hope and a future."

JEREMIAH 29:11 NIV

As Judah headed into exile, conquered by a
savage pagan people, God offered them hope.
He still had a good plan for them, one that
would come out of suffering. Their prosperity
was not at an end, though their path through
hardship had begun.

When God leads you up a rocky path,
your hope and future remain secure in Him.
Faithful trust is all He asks of you.

Go for It

When everything was hopeless,
Abraham believed anyway, deciding to
live...on what God said he would do.
ROMANS 4:18 MSG

"You can't do that. It's impossible." Have you ever been told this? Or just thought it because of fear or a previous experience with failure?

This world is full of those who discourage rather than encourage. If we believe them, we'll never do anything. But if we, like Abraham, believe that God has called us for a particular purpose, we'll go for it despite our track records. Past failure doesn't dictate future failure. If God wills it, He fulfills it.

Purposeful Plan

And we know that all things work together for good to those who love God, to those who are the called according to His purpose.

ROMANS 8:28 NKJV

Life doesn't always look ideal to us. When finances are tight, family problems are serious, or things just don't seem to go our way, we may doubt that God is working in our lives. That's the time we need to reread this verse and take heart. Even things that don't seem good have a purpose in God's plan. As Christians, we can trust in Him, even when life is less than perfect.

Heading Home

*We are only foreigners living
here on earth for a while.*

1 CHRONICLES 29:15 CEV

I quivered on the icy Alps peak, more from
fear than cold. Which ski slope was my level
(beginner) and which were treacherously
advanced? A mistake could be deadly. Panic
gripped me; I couldn't read the German signs
and no one spoke English.

As Christians, we're foreigners on this
earth. We don't speak the same language or
share the same perspective as nonbelievers.
We're only passing through this world on our
way to the next. . .heading home.

Open Door

"For God so loved the world that he gave his one and only Son, that whoever believes in him shall not perish but have eternal life."

JOHN 3:16 NIV

These words are God's open door to those who believe in His Son. The barrier between God's holiness and man's sinfulness disintegrates when we believe in Jesus' sacrifice for human sin. But we must walk through that open door, with faith, to inherit the eternal life God offers. Have you taken that step, or are you still outside the door?

I Do

Let us hold unswervingly to the hope we profess, for he who promised is faithful.
HEBREWS 10:23 NIV

An important part of any marriage is the vow of faithfulness. We pledge that we will remain faithful to our beloved until death do us part. Faithfulness is crucial to a trusting relationship. We must be able to depend on our spouse to always be in our corner, love us even when we're unlovable, and never leave or forsake us.

God is faithful. We can unswervingly depend on Him to never break His promises.

Gift of Love

The LORD takes delight in his people.
PSALM 149:4 NIV

God doesn't just like you—He delights in you.
You are so special to Him; He brought you into
His salvation so He could spend eternity with
you. God loves each of His children in a special
way. You aren't just another in a long line of
His people. He knows every bit of you, your
faithfulness and failures, and loves each part
of you "to pieces." We could never earn such
love—it is His special gift to each of us. Let's
rejoice in that blessing today.

Unfathomable Grace

Jesus treated us much better than we deserve. He made us acceptable to God and gave us the hope of eternal life.

TITUS 3:7 CEV

Whereas justice is getting what we deserve and mercy is not getting what we deserve, grace is getting what we don't deserve. Thankfully, God doesn't automatically dole out justice for our myriad sins, but reaches beyond to mercy and even a step further to grace. As Jean Valjean discovers in the classic story, *Les Miserables*, when we truly grasp God's unfathomable mercy and grace, we are then empowered to extend it to others.

God's Love Is at Work

We have known and believed the love that God has for us. God is love, and he who abides in love abides in God, and God in him.

1 JOHN 4:16 NKJV

Trusting in Jesus, you have felt God's love at work in your inner being. The vibrant connection that only Christians experience becomes the center of your life. If you are faithful, His eternal life renews you from head to toe and shines forth vibrantly. Your Spirit-inspired words and actions truly portray God's love to the world.

Roll Down the Window

> *"Ask and it will be given to you;
> seek and you will find; knock and
> the door will be opened to you."*
>
> LUKE 11:9 NIV

Does your fellow have trouble asking
directions? Do you cruise about the country
on a scenic tour that could have been avoided
by asking a simple question? We all find it
difficult to some degree when it comes to
asking for help. But that's how we reach
our final destinations—and not just on the
highway. God offers help if we only ask. He's
standing there holding the road map. We just
have to stop and roll down the window.

Endurance

As you know, we consider blessed those who have persevered. You have heard of Job's perseverance and have seen what the Lord finally brought about. The Lord is full of compassion and mercy.

JAMES 5:11 NIV

Endurance in faith, hard as it may seem, brings happiness. Trials are not a sign of God's disfavor or His will to carelessly punish His children. The tenderhearted Savior never acts cruelly. But through troubles, we draw close to Him and see God's power at work in our lives. Then, like Job, when we persevere in faith, God rewards us bountifully.

A New Tomorrow

Rahab the harlot. . .Joshua spared. . .
for she hid the messengers whom
Joshua sent to spy out Jericho.

JOSHUA 6:25 NASB

Rahab was the unlikeliest of heroes: a
prostitute who sold her body in the darkest
shadows. Yet she was the very person
God chose to fulfill His prophecy. How
astoundingly freeing! Especially for those of
us ashamed of our past. God loved Rahab for
who she was—not what she did. Rahab is
proof that God can and will use anyone for His
higher purposes. Anyone. Even you and me.

Mercy Triumphs

Mercy triumphs over judgment.

JAMES 2:13 NIV

Not only is God merciful to us, He expects us
to pass that blessing on to others. Instead of
becoming the rule enforcers in this world, He
wants us to paint a picture of the tender love
He has for fallen people and to call many other
sinners into His love. When we criticize the
world and do not show compassion, we lose
the powerful witness we were meant to have.
As you stand firm for Jesus, may mercy also
triumph in your life.

Name Above All Names

*O God, we give glory to you all day long and
constantly praise your name.*

PSALM 44:8 NLT

So what has God done that deserves our
everlasting praise? His descriptive names tell
the story: A friend that sticks closer than a
brother (Proverbs 18:24), Altogether lovely
(Song of Solomon 5:16), The rock that is
higher than I (Psalm 61:2), My strength and
my song (Isaiah 12:2), The lifter of my head
(Psalm 3:3), Shade from the heat (Isaiah 25:4).
His very name fills us with hope!

Rebirth and Renewal

*He saved us, not because of righteous things
we had done, but because of his mercy.
He saved us through the washing of rebirth
and renewal by the Holy Spirit.*

TITUS 3:5 NIV

———————

Could we save ourselves? No way! Even our
best efforts fall far short of God's perfection. If
God had left us on our own, we'd be eternally
separated from Him. But graciously, the
Father reached down to us through His Son,
sacrificing Jesus on the cross. Then the Spirit
touched our lives in rebirth and renewal.
Together the three Persons of the Godhead
saved us in merciful love.

Feel the Love

*Long before he laid down earth's
foundations, he had us in mind,
had settled on us as the focus of his love,
to be made whole and holy by his love.*

EPHESIANS 1:4 MSG

Need a boost of hope today? Read this
passage aloud, inserting your name for each
"us." Wow! Doesn't that bring home the
message of God's incredible, extravagant,
customized love for you? I am the focus of
His love, and I bask in the hope of healing,
wholeness, and holiness His individualized
attention brings. You too, dear sister, are His
focus. Allow yourself to feel the love today.

God Meets Our Needs

*"He has brought down rulers from their
thrones but has lifted up the humble.
He has filled the hungry with good things
but has sent the rich away empty."*

LUKE 1:52–53 NIV

God provides for every one of His children,
even the humblest. Wealth cannot gain His
favor nor poverty destroy it. The Father does
not look at the wallet, but at the heart. Those
who love Him, though they may lack cash, see
their needs fulfilled, but unbelievers who own
overflowing storehouses harvest empty hearts.
God never ignores His children's needs. What
has He given you today?

Seeking an Oasis

⊱⊰

*He changes a wilderness into a pool of water
and a dry land into springs of water.*
PSALM 107:35 NASB

The wilderness of Israel is truly a barren
wasteland—nothing but rocks and parched
sand stretching as far as the distant horizon.
The life-and-death contrast between stark
desert and pools of oasis water is startling.

Our lives can feel parched, too. Colorless.
Devoid of life. But God has the power to
transform desert lives into gurgling, spring-
of-water lives. Ask Him to bubble up springs
of hope within you today.

He Will Never Fail

*You open your hand and satisfy the
desires of every living thing.*

PSALM 145:16 NIV

Our faithful Lord provides for all His created
beings. Will He fail to care for you? How could
He satisfy the needs of the smallest birds and
beasts yet forget His human child? God is
always faithful. Though we fail, He will not.
He cannot forget His promises of love and will
never forget to provide for your every need.

Forever and Always

"Never will I leave you;
never will I forsake you."
HEBREWS 13:5 NIV

Unconditional love. We all yearn for it—from
our parents, our spouses, our children, our
friends. Love not based on our performance
or accomplishments, but on who we are
deep down beneath the fluff. God promises
unconditional love to those who honor Him.
We don't need to worry about disappointing
Him when He gets to know us better—He
knows us already. Better than we know
ourselves. And He loves us anyway, forever
and always.

His Gifts

If, by the trespass of the one man, death reigned through that one man, how much more will those who receive God's abundant provision of grace and of the gift of righteousness reign in life through the one man, Jesus Christ!

<small>ROMANS 5:17 NIV</small>

What greater gift could God give us than His grace? Once, death ruled over us. Now, life in Christ commands our days. As we ponder God's compassion, do we appreciate Christ's sacrifice? Any spiritual value we have comes from His gifts. We can never repay Him, but are we living to show how much we care?

Large and In Charge

❧❧❧

*"In this world you will have trouble.
But take heart! I have overcome the world."*

JOHN 16:33 NIV

"Who's in charge here?" Most mothers have
had the experience of returning home to a
chaos-wrecked house. Toys, books, clothes,
snack wrappers everywhere. "Why isn't
[insert correct answer here: your father, the
babysitter, Grandma, etc.] in control?"

Our world can sometimes feel chaotic
like that. Things appear to be spinning out of
control. But we must remember that God is
large and in charge. He has a plan.

Knowing God

In the beginning was the Word, and the Word was with God, and the Word was God.

JOHN 1:1 NIV

Want a picture of God's Word? Look at Jesus, the embodiment of everything the Father wanted to say to us. You can't do that if you don't read the Book that tells of Him.

Maybe that's why God takes it personally when we decide not to read His Word. We're ignoring His tender commands and pushing aside His love. God's scriptures communicate with His children. How can we know Him without His Word?

Only the Best

*I have hidden your word in my heart,
that I might not sin against you.*
PSALM 119:11 NLT

I adore homemade chicken salad. Honey
mustard, sliced grapes, and slivered almonds
make it delicious. Quality ingredients produce
quality results. It's all poultry, but there's
a big difference between white meat and
gizzards.

Memorizing scripture is like preparing
chicken salad for the soul. God's Word
(quality ingredients) will be ready at a
moment's notice to guide, comfort, and
train us in righteousness (quality results).
Anything else is just gizzards.

Flawless Words

"Every word of God is flawless."
PROVERBS 30:5 NIV

Maybe you've had days when you've been
tempted to doubt this verse. You wanted to go
in one direction, and God's Word said to go in
another. But if you were wise, you trusted in
its truth instead of following your own way.
After all, can you claim that your every word
is error-free? No. How much better to follow
in the perfect way of your Lord, who willingly
shares His wisdom. To avoid many of the
faults of this world, trust the flawless Word of
God.

Healing Heat

❧⦿❧

When I am weak, then I am strong.
2 CORINTHIANS 12:10 NASB

As an occupational therapist, I make splints for people with broken bones. The thermoplastic splinting material comes in sheets, hard and unyielding as plywood. When heated, the thermoplastic becomes pliable so it can be cut and molded into a form that promotes healing.

Like that thermoplastic, we're strongest and most usable when we've gone through the melting process. Heat transforms us into moldable beings with which God heals hearts and spirits.

The Light

❧

When Jesus spoke again to the people,
he said, "I am the light of the world.
Whoever follows me will never walk in
darkness, but will have the light of life."

JOHN 8:12 NIV

Following the light of the world means you
can see where you're headed. Even when life
becomes confusing and totally dark, your goal
hasn't changed, and you keep heading in the
right direction. Walking in Jesus' light, though
you hit a dark patch, you remain on the road
with the Savior, and in Him you always see
enough to take the next step.

Did You Say Something?

*"Call to Me and I will answer you,
and I will tell you great and mighty
things, which you do not know."*

JEREMIAH 33:3 NASB

As someone who's been there, done that,
you've gotta love the commercial where the
husband has his face buried in the newspaper
when his wife pops the no-win question:
"Does this dress make me look fat?" "You
bet," he distractedly replies.

God promises to not only hear us when
we call to Him, but to answer by teaching
us new and amazing things. He's never
distracted. He's always listening. And He
always cares.

Hope in Him

Put your hope in God, for I will yet praise him, my Savior and my God.

PSALM 42:5–6 NIV

Where else should the believer place her hope? No human has power to turn her life around without Jesus. No solution lies beyond Him, and He never pushes her away. When the world becomes harsh, she still receives His gentle encouragement.

Though you wait long and the path seems hard, hold on to Jesus. Words of praise will pass your lips as you see His salvation accomplished. Your God will never let you fall.

It's Not Over

When the wicked die, their hopes die
with them, for they rely on their
own feeble strength.

PROVERBS 11:7 NLT

Tony Dungy, Super Bowl champion, coach,
and author of *Quiet Strength*, said, "It's
because of God's goodness that we can have
hope, both for here and the hereafter."

Coach Dungy's testimony of eternal hope
for those who rely on God's infinite strength
touched many hearts after the tragic loss of
his teenage son. Death is not the end. There
is a hope, a future for those who choose to
not rely on their own feeble strength.

Be Strong

Be strong and take heart,
*all you who hope in the L*ord.
P*salm* 31:24 *niv*

Hope is not some weak, airy-fairy kind of
thing. It takes strength to put your trust
in God when life batters your heart and
soul. Weaklings rarely hold on to positive
expectation for long, because it takes too much
from them. But the spiritually strong put their
trust in God and let Him lift up their hearts in
hope. Then battering may come, but it cannot
destroy them. Hope makes Christians stronger
still.

Streets of Treats

❧⚜❧

*What you hope for is kept
safe for you in heaven.*
COLOSSIANS 1:5 CEV

Heaven. Will the streets really be paved with
gold? Or even better—chocolate? No, if our
earthly treasures are our source of security
and hope, we're in trouble. Rust, thieves,
decay, recession. . .things just aren't safe. But
peace? Joy? Reveling forever in our Lord's
presence? All waiting for us safely in heaven.
(But who says we can't hope for Godiva-
cobbled streets?)

Obedience = Joy

"I have told you this so that my joy may be in you and that your joy may be complete."

JOHN 15:11 NIV

What wouldn't we do to share Jesus' complete joy! But this verse comes after one of Jesus' commands to obedience. Ah, now do we change our minds? Does joy suddenly become impossible? When Jesus calls us to act, do we follow, or do we decide it's too hard and give up immediately? Let's keep our eyes on the outcome—the joy of our Lord filling our lives. Then obedience, too, may become a joy.

Justice Justice for All?

Our God, you save us, and your fearsome deeds answer our prayers for justice!
PSALM 65:5 CEV

It's not fair! How many times have we uttered this indignant cry when life handed us injustice? We demand justice—it's what we deserve, right? But what about all those times we've misstepped or misjudged? James 2:13 tells us that mercy triumphs over justice. Mercy forgives mistakes and doesn't dole out what is deserved. Mercy—like a jail sentence pardoned. Mercy—like a man on a cross.

Joy Will Come

*My lips will shout for joy when I sing praise
to you—I, whom you have delivered.*
PSALM 71:23 NIV

Having trouble finding joy in your life today?
Do what the psalmists often did and remind
yourself what God has already done for you.
How many ways has following Him blessed
you? Begin by thanking Him for His saving
grace, and the joy starts, no matter what you
face today. Your lips will show the delight in
your heart.

Smiling Hearts

Weeping may last for the night,
but a shout of joy comes in the morning.
PSALM 30:5 NASB

What woman hasn't seen the dim underbelly of 2 a.m. through hot tears? God gave us emotionally sensitive spirits and is willing to sit with us as we weep through the long, hard night. Sometimes "night" lasts for a season. But He promises that the sun will eventually rise. And on that glorious morning, we'll be filled with so much joy, even our hearts will smile. Joy is appreciated most in the wake of disappointment.

Close to Jesus

"Be still, and know that I am God."
PSALM 46:10 NIV

———————————————

So often, we seek to do things for God or to
prove our Christian witness. But if we become
simply caught up in busyness, we lose the
distinction of our faith: a close relationship
with Jesus. Knowing God is not about what we
do, but whom we love. Our good works mean
little if we disconnect from Him. Spend time
being still with God today, and a deepened
knowledge of Him will be your blessing.

Who's Your Daddy?

His name is the Lord. . . .
A father to the fatherless.
Psalm 68:4–5 niv

His father left when my friend Ben was two.
Ben recognized him once—from pictures—at
a family funeral, but his father intentionally
turned away. When Ben was thirty-five, with
a family of his own, his father suddenly
showed up, seeking a relationship. Sadly,
he was diagnosed with cancer shortly after
their reunion and died within one year.
Ben mourned but knew his real paternal
relationship was with God, the Father to the
fatherless.

Know Him Intimately

"I will take you as my own people, and I will be your God. Then you will know that I am the LORD your God, who brought you out from under the yoke of the Egyptians."

EXODUS 6:7 NIV

God freed the Hebrews from slavery and brought them to their new land. But He didn't stop there. Today He still proves Himself to people by freeing them from sin's slavery and creating loving relationships with them. Has God freed you from sin? Then know Him intimately. Draw near and enjoy His blessings, no matter what "slavery" you've faced before.

Fresh and Green

They will still bear fruit in old age,
they will stay fresh and green.
PSALM 92:14 NIV

Doris, a tiny ninety-year-old widow in my
Bible study, is teaching me how to be a
blessing. That's her prayer every morning
of her life: Lord, make me a blessing to
someone today. And sure enough, God uses
her to touch lives in His name—helping a
frantic woman find her lost keys; taking a sick
neighbor to the doctor; offering a friendly
word to the grumpy, wheelchair-bound man.
Little blessings are big indeed to those in
need.

Father and Son

We know also that the Son of God has come and has given us understanding, so that we may know him who is true. And we are in him who is true by being in his Son Jesus Christ. He is the true God and eternal life.

1 JOHN 5:20 NIV

How do we know God? Through His Son, Jesus, who helps us understand the love of His Father. There is no space, no difference of opinion, between Father and Son. When we know the Son, we know God truly. Trust in one is trust in both.

Superwoman Isn't Home

*"But we will devote ourselves to prayer
and to the ministry of the word."*
ACTS 6:4 NASB

As busy women, we've found out the hard
way that we can't do everything. Heaven
knows we've tried, but the truth has found
us out: Superwoman is a myth. So we must
make priorities and focus on the most
important. Prayer and God's Word should
be our faith priorities. If we only do as much
as we can do, then God will take over and
do what only He can do. He's got our backs,
girls!

Perfecting Our Love

❦

Jesus replied: " 'Love the Lord your God with all your heart and with all your soul and with all your mind.' "

MATTHEW 22:37 NIV

This simple command can be a real challenge, can't it? No matter how we try, in our own power, to love God completely, we always seem to fail somewhere. Only as God's Spirit works in our hearts will our whole being become ever more faithful. God works in us day by day, perfecting our love. Ask Him to help you love Him today.

He is Able

The prospect of the righteous is joy.
PROVERBS 10:28 NIV

Living joyfully isn't denying reality. The righteous do not receive a "Get Out of Pain Free" card when they place their trust in Christ. We all have hurts in our lives. Some we think we cannot possibly endure. But even in the midst of our darkest times, our heavenly Father is able to reach in with gentle fingers to touch us and infuse us with joy that defies explanation. Impossible? Perhaps by the world's standards. Yet He is able.

Gentle Reminder

If a man say, I love God, and hateth his brother, he is a liar: for he that loveth not his brother whom he hath seen, how can he love God whom he hath not seen?

1 JOHN 4:20 KJV

John's letter surely knows how to challenge us. Now we wonder, *Do I love God at all?* Surely, on our own, we couldn't. But when we accept God and receive His love, our attitude changes. In Jesus we can love even a bothersome brother. Sometimes we just need a gentle reminder.

Lighthouse Love

For God, who said, "Light shall shine out of darkness," is the One who has shone in our hearts.

2 CORINTHIANS 4:6 NASB

Have you heard the story of the lighthouse keeper's daughter who kept faithful vigil for her sailor? Every night she watched as the light's beam pierced the blackness and sliced through raging storms, driven by relentless hope that her lover would return to her on the morning's tide. God loves us like that. He's our light in the darkness: guiding, beckoning, and filling our hearts with hope. He never tires. He never stops.

New Life

Therefore, if anyone is in Christ, he is a new creation; old things have passed away; behold, all things have become new.

2 CORINTHIANS 5:17 NKJV

New life in Christ: What indescribable freedom to be separated from our sin! No longer bound by it but able to live in Him, we joyfully race into our new existence.

But in time, our tendency to fall into sin tarnishes God's gift. Suddenly we don't feel so new. "Old" Christians need only turn again to Christ for forgiveness, and the Spirit's cleansing makes us new again.

That Morning

You have placed your faith and hope in God because he raised Christ from the dead and gave him great glory.

1 PETER 1:21 NLT

Have you ever wondered how Mary felt that Easter morning when she discovered Jesus' tomb empty? Already grieving, imagine the shock of discovering the body of her Savior—the One who held all her hopes and dreams—gone! How can that be? Maybe. . . ? Hope glimmers. But no—impossible. He did say something about resurrection, but that was figurative, wasn't it? *Who are. . . You are? I must run and tell them. It's true! He has risen! He's alive! My hope lives, too!*

Celebrate Your Newness

If Christ is in you, the body is dead because of sin, but the Spirit is life because of righteousness.

ROMANS 8:10 NKJV

Know Jesus? Then your body and your fleshly desires are less important than your spirit. Because Jesus lives in you, sin has no permanent claim on your life. Though it tempts you and you may give in for a time, it no longer has a firm grasp on all your days. You can turn aside from it and dwell in your Lord instead. Celebrate your newness in Jesus: live for Him today!

Walkin' Boots

I heard about you from others;
now I have seen you with my own eyes.
JOB 42:5 CEV

A s children we sang, "Jesus loves me, this
I know; for the Bible tells me so," and we
believed because, well, we were told to. But
we reach a crossroads as adults: Either pull
on the boots of faith and take ownership or
simply polish them occasionally—maybe at
Easter and Christmas—and allow them to sit
neglected and dusty in the closet. Have you
taken ownership of your faith? Go ahead,
sister, those boots were made for walkin'!

Don't Be Afraid to Ask

Brothers and sisters, pray for us.
1 THESSALONIANS 5:25 NIV

Do you find it hard to ask others to pray for you? Don't be afraid to take that step into humility. Paul wasn't when he asked the Thessalonians to pray for his ministry. Being part of the church requires an interdependence of prayers given and received. As a congregation prays for each other, their spirits connect in a new, caring way. Choose carefully those with whom you share private concerns, but never fear to ask a mature Christian to pray for you.

Labor

❧⊱⊰❧

We call to mind your work of faith,
your labor of love, and your patience
of hope in following our Master,
Jesus Christ, before God our Father.

1 Thessalonians 1:3 msg

Labor. The word alone draws a shudder from
the most stalwart of pregnant women. Just
as laboring to bring forth new physical life
requires patience, birthing new spiritual
life may require an intensive labor of love:
ceaseless prayer. Countless women on their
knees praying for the salvation of a loved
one have rejoiced in answered prayer. Their
secret? Patience of hope.

The Best Answer

Pray without ceasing.
1 THESSALONIANS 5:17 KJV

Haven't gotten an answer to your prayer?
Don't give up. There's no time limit on
speaking to God about your needs. It's
just that we often work on a different time
schedule from God. We want an answer
yesterday, while He has something better in
mind for tomorrow. So keep praying. God
listens to His children and gives them the best
answer, not the fastest one.

Essential Trio

Love is patient, love is kind.
1 CORINTHIANS 13:4 NIV

Love, patience, and kindness go together. In fact, it's hard to imagine love that would not express itself in both patience and kindness! That's because even intense, God-sent love for the people in your life does not protect you from feeling annoyed with them or exasperated by their actions from time to time. Yet true love prompts you to respond with patience, not intolerance, as they struggle through their weaknesses. True love compels you to treat them with kindness, not malice, when they upset or offend you. Love, patience, kindness—three must-haves for strong, healthy, and lasting relationships

Blessing behind Repentance

"Repent, then, and turn to God, so that your sins may be wiped out, that times of refreshing may come from the Lord."
ACTS 3:19 NIV

When we consider repentance, we tend to think it's hard. That's only because we're shortsighted. Giving up sin may not appeal to our hardened hearts because we're not looking at the blessing set behind repentance. Yet as we turn from sin, we feel the refreshing breath of God's Spirit bringing new life to our lives. Then, does anything seem difficult?

Wait Just a Minute

We wait in hope for the LORD;
he is our help and our shield.
PSALM 33:20 NIV

Impatience: archenemy of women. Like
Batman's Riddler, or Superman's Lex Luthor,
impatience stalks us, plots our demise, and
blindsides us via thoughtless neighbors,
inconsiderate drivers, careless clerks, dense
husbands, children taking *for–ev–er*. But
waiting is an unavoidable part of life, and the
Bible says we don't have to be undone by it.
The Lord's patience is our shield and defense,
and He's got plenty stockpiled.

In His Power

I can do all things through
Christ who strengthens me.
PHILIPPIANS 4:13 NKJV

Need strength? Turn to God for all you need.
Why take on life by yourself when He offers
all you need? Often, as obedient Christians,
we make great efforts with our feeble spiritual
muscles. But ultimately our own strength
always fails. When Christ's Spirit works
through us, the Christian life flows smoothly;
in His power we accomplish His purposes.
Today is Christ bearing the burden, or are we?
Only He has the might we need in our lives.

Sprouts

"For there is hope for a tree, when it is cut down, that it will sprout again."

JOB 14:7 NASB

Have you ever battled a stubborn tree? You know, one you can saw off at the ground but the tenacious thing keeps sprouting new growth from the roots? You have to admire the resiliency of that life force, struggling in its refusal to give up. That's hope in a nutshell, sisters. We must believe, even as stumps, that we will eventually become majestic, towering evergreens if we just keep sending out those sprouts.

You Will Prosper

"But you shall meditate in it [the Book of the Law] day and night. . .do not turn from it. . .that you may prosper."

JOSHUA 1:8, 7 NKJV

God promised success to Joshua if he obeyed His Word. That promise works for you, too. But sometimes you may not feel that obeying God has brought you great prosperity. Just wait. It may take time, the success may not take the form you expect, or you may not see the results until you reach heaven, but God will prosper those who do His will. He promised it, and His promises never fail.

Getting to Know You

*For the law never made anything perfect.
But now we have confidence in a better hope,
through which we draw near to God.*

HEBREWS 7:19 NLT

Following Old Testament law used to be considered the way to achieve righteousness, but obeying rules just doesn't work for fallible humans. We mess up. We fail miserably. Then Jesus came and provided a better way to draw near to God. He bridged the gap by offering us a personal relationship rather than rules. Together we laugh, cry, love, grieve, rejoice. We get to know our Papa God through our personal relationship with Him.

Real Success

Save now, we beseech You, O Lord;
send now prosperity, O Lord,
we beseech You, and give to us success!
PSALM 118:25 AMP

Is it wrong to pray for success? No. But notice
that the Bible connects success to God's
salvation. Prosperity or any other achievement
means little when it's separated from God's
will and our obedience to Him. When you
ask to attain something, do you also seek
God's saving grace in that part of your life?
If so, you'll have real success—spiritual and
temporal blessings.

Nothing More than Feelings

*LORD, sustain me as you promised,
that I may live! Do not let
my hope be crushed.*
PSALM 119:116 NLT

Whatever our foe—unemployment, rejection, loss, illness—we may feel beaten down by life. Hope feels crushed by the relentless boulder bearing down on our souls. We feel that we can't possibly endure another day. Yes, we feel, we feel. But feelings are often deceiving. God promises to sustain us, to strengthen us, so that we might withstand that massive rock. We can trust Him. He will not allow us to be crushed!

Lean on Jesus

*"Therefore if the Son makes you free,
you shall be free indeed."*

JOHN 8:36 NKJV

Sometimes we don't feel freed from sin.
Temptations draw us, even though we
love Jesus. So His words here can be both
comforting and challenging. The Jews wanted
to trust in their spiritual history, not God.
That plan didn't work well for them, and it
won't work for us either. We can't rely on
history or our past deeds to put sin behind us.
What will work? Leaning on Jesus every day,
trusting Him to make us free indeed!

Redeemed!

O Israel, hope in the LORD; for with the LORD
there is lovingkindness, and with Him
is abundant redemption.

PSALM 130:7 NASB

The psalmist knew Israel had a rotten track
record. Throughout Old Testament history,
God miraculously delivered the Israelites
from trouble repeatedly, and they would
gratefully turn to Him, only to eventually
slip again into rebellion and more trouble.
Sounds a lot like you and me, doesn't it? But
thankfully, ours is a redemptive God; a God
who offers abundant loving-kindness and
forgiveness. A God of second chances—then
and now.

Appreciation Overflow

Continue to live in [Jesus], rooted and
built up in him, strengthened in
the faith as you were taught,
and overflowing with thankfulness.
COLOSSIANS 2:6–7 NIV

Strong Christians are thankful Christians. As
we realize all Jesus has sacrificed for us and
appreciate our inability to live the Christian
life on our own, we remember to praise our
Savior for His grace. Today we can be rooted in
Jesus, strong in our faith, and thankful to the
One who has given us these blessings. Let's
overflow with appreciation!

Mr. Clean for the Soul

᙭᙭᙭

*As far as the east is from the west, so far has
He removed our transgressions from us.*

PSALM 103:12 NASB

———————————

Dirty little secrets. We all have them. Exposing
them is a popular theme for television shows
these days. But we don't have to wallow in the
muck of our past. God has promised to wash
us clean of our dirty little secrets and remove
them as far as the east is from the west when
we repent of our wrongdoings and ask him
for forgiveness. An immaculate and sparkling
fresh start—redemption is Mr. Clean for the
soul!

Wonderful Thanks

Oh, give thanks to the LORD, for He is good!
For His mercy endures forever.
PSALM 136:1 NKJV

Now, honestly, how do you respond to this
call for thanks? Does your heart leap at the
opportunity, or does it just hit you with a dull
thud? Why is it so important to thank God?
Because He will always be merciful to you.
Whether you rejoice easily or hit the floor with
a thud, if you have trusted in the Savior, He
still loves you. Isn't that something wonderful
to give thanks for?

Counting on It

❧

*Blessed is the one who perseveres under trial,
because having stood the test, that person
will receive the crown of life that the Lord
has promised to those who love him.*

JAMES 1:12 NIV

Some think that when you turn your life over
to Christ, troubles are over. But if you've been
a believer for more than a day, you'll realize
that the Christian life is no Caribbean cruise.
There will be trials; there will be tribulations.
Count on it. But Jesus promises a glorious
reward for our perseverance through those
hard times. Count on that even more.

God Calls Us to Joy

Consider it pure joy, my brothers and sisters,
whenever you face trials of many kinds.

JAMES 1:2 NIV

Joy? To be faced with trials should cause us
joy? Hard to imagine, isn't it? But God calls
us to joy when unbelievers persecute us
because of our faith or when our situation is
merely difficult. It is a joy to Him that we have
stood firm in faith, and He calls us to share
His delight. That doesn't mean we seek out
trials, but that we face the situation hand in
hand with God. In trials our spiritual strength
increases.

Overflowing Love

Precious in the sight of the LORD
is the death of His godly ones.
PSALM 116:15 NASB

Jesus wept. Two small words that portray the
enormity of Jesus' emotion following the
death of His dear friend, Lazarus (John 11:35).
Jesus knew Lazarus wouldn't stay dead, that
he'd soon miraculously rise from the grave.
So why did Jesus weep? The depth of His
love for those precious to Him overflowed.
Our Lord grieves with us in our losses today
and comforts us with the knowledge that His
beloved will rise to eternal life in heaven.

His Concern

The righteous cry out, and the LORD hears,
and delivers them out of all their troubles.
PSALM 34:17 NKJV

As God's child, you have His ear 24/7 if only
you will pray. Every need, trouble, or praise is
His concern. And not only will He hear about
your trials, He will deliver you from them. Feel
discouraged in your troubles? You need not
stay that way. Just spend time with Jesus. His
help is on the way.

Guilt-Free

*"I will forgive their wickedness,
and I will never again remember their sins."*
HEBREWS 8:12 NLT

Guilt. It tends to consume us women to the
point that 90 percent of the things we do are
motivated by guilt. But God says we don't
have to allow guilt to control us. We should
learn from past mistakes, certainly, and then
shed the guilt like a moth-eaten winter coat.
Don a fresh spring outfit and look ahead. Our
past prepares us for the future if we are open
to the present.

God's Compassionate Salvation

*Do not repay anyone evil for evil. Be careful
to do what is right in the eyes of everyone.*

ROMANS 12:17 NIV

Tit-for-tat retribution for evil is not a principle
of our compassionate God. We understand this
if we've received His undeserved salvation.
With such a gift, God has opened our hearts
to treating our enemies as He has treated us.
If we fail to count up each wrong and repay
it with harshness, lost souls may understand
God's compassionate salvation. By doing right,
even when we receive wrong in return, we
become powerful witnesses.

Close to You

I stay close to you,
and your powerful arm supports me.
PSALM 63:8 CEV

There's an old saying: "I used to be close to God, but someone moved." If God is the same yesterday, today, and tomorrow, He's not the one going anywhere. So how do we stay close to God? So close that His powerful arm supports, protects, and lifts us up when we're down? Prayer: as a lifestyle, as much a part of ourselves as breathing. Prayer isn't just spiritual punctuation; it's every word of our life story.

A Real Gift

❧✦❧

Believe in the Lord Jesus,
and you will be saved.

ACTS 16:31 NIV

A genuine gift doesn't cost you a cent. It's
given to you because the giver loves you and
wants to make you happy. Who would insult
such a gracious person by pulling out money
to pay for the gift? Yet that's what happens
when godly acts are done to earn salvation!
It's trying to pay for the gift of love God has
given to you solely because He delights in you
and desires to fill your heart with joy. Doing
good—not to earn His gift, but to thank Him
for it—provides your Spirit-given motivation
for your many kindnesses to others.

Raising Our Hopes

"Did I ask you for a son, my lord?" she said.
"Didn't I tell you, 'Don't raise my hopes'?"
2 KINGS 4:28 NIV

Are you afraid to raise your hope in God's
provision for fear that hope will crash
and burn? The woman from Shunem had
everything but her heart's desire—a child. She
was afraid to believe Elisha's prediction of
her pregnancy, but his prayerful intervention
made her dream come true. When the boy
later died, however, she lashed out. God
restored her son and raised her hope from the
dead. Literally. Dare we raise our hopes, too?

Source of Salvation

*He became the source of eternal salvation
for all who obey him.*

HEBREWS 5:9 NIV

Salvation in Jesus is important to our earthly
lives. How many times has He dispelled
danger or helped us avoid it? How often has
sin failed to mar our lives because we obeyed
His commands? But Jesus is also the source
of salvation in eternity. Instead of remaining
forever in our earthly lives, God planned to
bring us into everlasting life with Him, in His
restored kingdom. In heaven, we will praise
His salvation, without end.

Scripture Index